TALES

FROM

THE

TIMES

TALES
FROM
THE
TIMES

Real-Life Stories to Make You Think, Wonder,
and Smile, from the Pages of *The New York Times*

THE STAFF OF *THE NEW YORK TIMES*

EDITED BY LISA BELKIN

 ST. MARTIN'S GRIFFIN   NEW YORK

www.stmartins.com

Design by Phil Mazzone

Library of Congress Cataloging-in-Publication Data

Tales from the times : real-life stories to make you think, wonder, and smile, from the pages of The New York Times / staff of The New York Times ; edited by Lisa Belkin.—1st St. Martin's Griffin ed.
    p. cm.
  ISBN 0-312-31233-4
  I. Belkin, Lisa, 1960–   II. New York Times.
  AC8.T165 2004
  081—dc22

                                                        2003018030

First Edition: April 2004

10 9 8 7 6 5 4 3 2 1

To Eliza and Jake,
Evan and Alex,
and Caitlin

CONTENTS

ACKNOWLEDGMENTS   ix

A NOTE FROM THE EDITOR   xi

CHANGING LIVES   1

ANIMALS   43

SCHOOL   77

SPORTS   107

FAMILIES   155

LANGUAGE   181

FARAWAY PLACES   197

CLOSER TO HOME   221

TRYING TO GET ALONG   257

ACKNOWLEDGMENTS

THIS BOOK WOULD NOT EXIST without Glenn Kramon, who had the idea in the first place and was tireless about making that idea happen. It would also not exist if Mike Levitas and Susan Chira at the *Times*, and George Witte and Elizabeth Bewley at St. Martin's Press, had not taken on Glenn's vision as their own and seen it through.

While collecting and editing the selections in this anthology, I was struck anew at the depth of talent within the pages of *The New York Times*. If not for the paper's remarkable collection of writers and editors, with their eye for detail, and their wondrous way with words, there could also be no book.

Particular thanks to Nick Kristof, Sam Howe Verhovek, Sara Rimer, and Peter Applebome, who answered the call and searched their own memories and archives for the perfect tales. To Maureen

ACKNOWLEDGMENTS

Balleza, who made possible all the stories of mine that are included here. To Laura Jin Joo Lambert, researcher par excellence, who found gem after gem with patience and panache. And to Michael Shapiro, for sending me Laura.

A Note from the Editor

TALES FROM THE TIMES **BEGAN** at a backyard barbecue, when a group *New York Times* reporters and editors found that they were all in the habit of tucking their children in at bedtime by telling them stories from the newspaper.

These were not just any stories. They were Tales. Those wonderful, luscious, rollicking good dramas that make our paper more than just a chronicle of what happened yesterday. The kinds of stories that teach us not only about others, but about ourselves; that make us nod in recognition, or find us marveling at what we never knew existed.

The story of a food editor who befriends a chicken in his Queens backyard. A delivery man who befriends a beggar and helps him find his way back home.

A child prodigy who learns physics when she is only 10 years old. A thief in Rome who steals 1,000 euros from the bottom of an outdoor fountain.

Twins separated at birth who find each other accidentally at college. A 5-year-old boy who takes his mother's car because his baby sister wants a ride to the beach.

As we told our children these tales, we simplified them here and there, so that the drama and the message took center stage. We've simplified them in this book, too, and as we did this we saw that these are not stories just for children, but for all of us who savor a true tale deftly told.

Taken together, these stories provide a glimpse of the world, which, we realized, was the magical point we were trying to share during all those storytelling bedtimes. By gathering the tales together, we can take those glimpses out of newsprint and onto bookshelves, helping them to live on beyond the news. We can hold these slices of reality—which are both a mirror of life and larger than life— between two covers, where, like any good story, we can read them again and again.

CHANGING LIVES

Friends Who Met on the Street

NEW YORK, N.Y.—Vincent Jones cannot forget the first time he saw the homeless man. He was so skinny and weak, Mr. Jones says, he was "holding up his pants with one hand and holding on to the wall with the other."

That first time, Mr. Jones remembers, a police officer was yelling at the man, telling him he had to leave the small square of sidewalk he called home. Mr. Jones kept walking that day, but a few days later something drew him back—something he still finds hard to explain. "The look on that man's face," he says now.

The man, Raymond Lawrence, asked Mr. Jones for a quarter. Mr. Jones gave him two. He also bought him a cup of coffee and a bacon-and-egg sandwich. He asked the man—please—not to spend his money on alcohol, and then he walked away, sure he would never see him again. That was three years ago. A lot has happened since.

Mr. Jones is a delivery man. His truck route often took him past the place where Mr. Lawrence stood each day and begged for money and food. Slowly Mr. Jones began to become part of Mr. Lawrence's life. Over the months the delivery man learned that the homeless man had been in the Navy, had lived as far away as Alaska, and had once been a talented jazz pianist. He learned that the homeless man had a family who he had not seen in many years.

Mr. Jones was worried about the homeless man. He was sick and dirty from years of living on the streets. He was often beaten and robbed by other street people. One winter his shoes were stolen and his toes became frozen. Surgeons operated and the city bought him a shiny new wheelchair, but it was stolen within a week. "There were times when I said to myself: 'I am going to watch this man die out here,'" Mr. Jones said. Which is why he decided to help Mr. Lawrence find his way back home.

Years of alcohol had scarred Mr. Lawrence's memory, but he gave Mr. Jones some clues here and there. Using them, Mr. Jones discovered that one of Mr. Lawrence's sisters, Mary Helen, worked in New York City and regularly got off the bus right near the spot where Mr. Jones slept on the sidewalk. He also discovered that Mr. Lawrence's mother was still living in Virginia, near the town where Mr. Lawrence was born. And he had another sister—Cathaleen—living in Boston. Amazingly, Mr. Jones even remembered her telephone number.

So Mr. Jones called that sister, who immediately put him in touch with her mother, who had not heard from her son for more than three years. One morning soon after that, Mr. Jones walked up to Mr. Lawrence on his patch of sidewalk. Mr. Jones held out a cellphone and told the homeless man that his mother was on the phone.

Mr. Lawrence looked at the phone and then said into it, tears welling in his eyes: "Is this really my mother?"

The voice of a woman, crying, shot back: "On October 3, 1948, they handed me a baby and told me it was you, so I guess it's your mother, Raymond."

That was the turning point.

Mr. Jones was so excited he wanted to drive Mr. Lawrence to Virginia the next day. But first he got him a haircut and a new set of clothes and a dinner of baked chicken, corn, potatoes and peas.

The drive to Virginia took ten hours, and it was evening when they arrived at the small, white shingled house where Mr. Lawrence's mother lived. She walked out the front door with tears streaming down her face, as she took her son into her arms.

For all the years he was missing, she said, she's looked for him wherever she went. "It's a wonder I wasn't killed," she said. "Because every time I saw someone on the street, any skinny little man walking along the side of the road, I would wonder if it was Raymond, and I would turn to look real hard, and I would nearly run into something and kill myself."

Randy Kennedy

One year later, Vincent Jones went back down to Virginia to visit Raymond Lawrence. The reporter, Randy Kennedy, went along, too, and this is what he wrote:

PORTSMOUTH, Va.—Some things about Raymond Lawrence have changed hardly at all in the last year. He is still as thin as a pool cue, his fingers long and spindly. He still gets uncomfortably quiet and stares straight ahead when people start talking too much about his past. He still walks slowly and with a limp, because of the missing toes that frostbite stole from him on the streets of Manhattan not so long ago.

But some things have changed a lot.

Now he has a home—in the tiny bedroom off the living room in his mother's house. And he has not had an alcoholic drink—even though, like most alcoholics, he fights the desire to drink almost every day. He has learned to drive, and scored a perfect test on his Virginia driver's test.

Perhaps most important of all, he is playing the piano again. At first his fingers trembled, and his memory failed him, but now his playing is beautiful and poetic and secure. He has a job, too, as assistant music director at a nearby church, and has not missed a service since he began.

On a recent Saturday afternoon, a reporter went to visit Mr. Lawrence and his mother, accompanied by Mr. Jones, who had also not seen the man he calls "my buddy Raymond" for an entire year. Mrs. Lawrence was in the midst of making dinner—barbecue chicken, collard greens, rice—and the house was filled with the warm smell of food. Mr. Lawrence, glasses perched on the end of his nose, was poring over some songs for a church service the next morning.

The tiny living room, where one keyboard sat last year, is now dominated by two large keyboards and two bulky black amplifiers that take up more room than the couch. "If I didn't stop him," said his mother, "Raymond would have keyboards stacked up to the ceiling in here."

That Saturday, as the three sat together again, they seemed to forget their troubles. Mr. Lawrence, who rarely lets anyone see how he is feeling, hugged Mr. Jones as he squeezed through the door. "Look at you!" Mr. Jones said. "Just look at you, Raymond. You look fine."

The two men began to talk like old friends, about deer hunting, horse racing and truck driving—the last of which Mr. Lawrence had done for a living in more states than he can now remember. Mr. Lawrence, who never laughed when he lived on the streets because there was little to laugh at, was joking and smiling.

And then, as he always seems to do when company comes over, Mr. Lawrence sat down to play the piano. The year before, at church, Mr. Jones had asked his friend to play his favorite hymn, "Pass Me Not, O Gentle Savior." Mr. Lawrence remembered and began to play it once more, his back curved over the keyboard, his eyes clenched shut, as if in a trance.

A 5-Year-Old's Wild Ride

PORT CHESTER, N.Y.—Sometimes a guy like Rocco Morabito just feels like hitting the road.

So at about 7 A.M. yesterday, the young man borrowed his mom's car, picked up his baby sister, and set off down the highway.

His only problem was seeing over the steering wheel.

Two-and-a-half miles from his home, Rocco, 5 years old, was pulled over by a police officer concerned that his tan Buick station wagon—which was obeying all traffic rules—appeared to be driverless.

"It looked like the Invisible Man was driving that car," said Anthony J. Schembri, the Police Commissioner of Rye, where the car was stopped.

Officer Robert P. Vogel caught up with Rocco's car, which was maneuvering through rush-hour traffic on Midland Avenue at about 20 miles an hour.

"I observed that the car was being driven pretty well," he said. "But all I could see was a small girl standing in the back seat."

At first he wasn't sure how to stop a car that was driving itself. "What was running through my mind was: Do I turn on my lights and siren?" he said. "Do I pull in front and try to stop it?" Finally, he said, he tried the lights and siren, "and the car pulls over to the curb, in perfect accordance with the laws of New York State."

Rocco, wearing pajamas and sneakers, and his 2-year-old sister, Brandi, in just a pajama top, began to cry. Rocco climbed out without disengaging the car's engine, forcing Officer Vogel to reach into the rolling vehicle and take it out of gear.

The police said family members told them that Rocco's mother was ill and his father was working when Rocco took the keys from his mother's purse, opened the garage door, backed out and began his adventure.

They said Rocco had pulled the automatic seat all the way forward and, at about three feet tall, he could just touch the accelerator.

The young motorist's run-in with the police did not dim his love for the road.

"I told them their mommy would have to come get them," Officer Vogel said, "but the kid says, 'My mommy can't come here because I have the only car. I can drive. I'll go get her.'"

Mark A. Uhlig

Eleven years later, Rocco was finally old enough to drive legally. When he went out for a drive, reporter John Tierney went with him.

Rocco Morabito finally drove his sister all the way to the beach. He was safe at last from the police, thanks to the learner's permit he got on his 16th birthday, and he handled the car even better than he had the first time.

"It's easier when you can see over the top of the steering wheel," he explained as he pulled out of the garage, navigating the same narrow driveway where his famous ride began the morning of Dec. 4, 1987.

Rocco was front-page news ("JUNIOR JOY RIDE") in New York City, after that, and for a while his ride was better known internationally than Paul Revere's. Well-wishers and automotive companies showered him with cards and gifts. He was interviewed by David Letterman and countless journalists, who happily reported his ambition to become a truck driver. His best media moment came when he was asked on A *Current Affair* if he had learned any lesson from the experience.

"Yes," he replied. "I learned how to drive."

Actually, he'd had a little practice beforehand, because his grandfather had let Rocco sit in his lap and drive the car around a parking lot. But it still took remarkable initiative to make off with the car. "We always knew he was a smart, observant kid," said his mother, Susan Morabito. "He'd carefully watch everything you did. But we never imagined he could figure out how to take the car. I almost had a heart attack when they called me."

Rocco remembers that he'd gotten the car keys by standing on a chair to reach his mother's purse on top of the refrigerator. He opened the garage door, put his sister in the back seat and buckled her seat belt. Then he moved the automatic front seat all the way forward and the steering wheel all the way down. He set off, carefully avoiding the wall lining the driveway.

"It was raining, so I stopped in the driveway to turn on the windshield wipers," he recalled. "I knew how to do that from watching my dad. Then I pulled out of the driveway and watched for other cars. I could just see over the dashboard if I looked through the steering wheel."

As he retraced the route yesterday along Midland Avenue, he pointed out the stoplights where he'd dutifully observed the law, and recalled the little drama at the intersection with Peck Avenue.

"When I was stopped at this light," he said, "a man came up to me and said: 'You're not supposed to be driving. Get out of the car.' He tried to reach in and turn off the engine, but I hit the power window. As the window was rolling up, I started to drive away. He got his hand caught for a moment and then let go."

But it was only a temporary escape, because the man found Officer Vogel in a nearby deli and sent him in pursuit of the two outlaws.

"We were really scared when he pulled us over," Rocco said. "My sister tried hiding under the back seat. I slid over to the passenger's seat to pretend I hadn't been driving."

Alas, Officer Vogel was on to them.

Yesterday, after safely conducting his family's new station wagon to the beach at Rye Playland, Rocco said he still found driving exciting, but confessed that he had set aside his truck-driving ambitions. As a junior at Port Chester High School, he plays on the football and baseball teams, and is hoping to get a sports scholarship to college. "I'd love to play professional sports," he said.

As they looked out at the water yesterday, Rocco and Brandi still couldn't explain exactly what came over them that morning in 1987. "I've been asked over and over why I did it," Rocco said, "but I don't know. The only reason I can think of is that my sister wanted to go to the beach."

A Long Journey to Where?

FLORENCE, Ariz.—It appears that Reza K. Baluchi made a string of serious miscalculations.

One, an adviser might say, never cross the Mexican border illegally, especially if you are from Iran.

Two, if you do cross, don't pitch a tent in the Arizona desert.

Three, if people want to bail you out of jail, do not stop them.

The abridged version of Mr. Baluchi's fantastic tale goes something like this: He escapes from his country, Iran, on a bicycle and sets out on a 46,000-mile trip around the globe. It is a trip, he says, to bring world peace.

Over the next six years, he visits some of the nastiest, roughest, poorest, unhappiest, corners of the planet—lands of starvation and war and discontent. Yet there is something so kind and charming about him that wherever he goes people welcome him. Peasants give him food. Leaders give him presents and well-wishes. A Colombian dentist even fixes his teeth without charge. In all, Mr. Baluchi pedals his bicycle over six continents and 54 countries.

But the story ends here in the United States when Mr. Baluchi is found camping in the Arizona desert by a Border Patrol helicopter and is arrested for entering the country without permission.

So now he lives at a government detention facility here in Florence. He runs circles around the exercise yard, quite certain that when the immigration judge hears this story, the judge will be overcome by a profound sense of humanity and release him. And when he is released, Mr. Baluchi says, he will resume the final leg of his ride. His destination? Ground Zero, New York City.

"My religion is peace," Mr. Baluchi said in Farsi and broken English. "I no like terrorist. I for peace. All people Iran. U.S.A. New York."

Exactly what Mr. Baluchi was doing on the American side of the border is a matter of interpretation. He explains that he simply got lost while riding around Mexico, where he had been waiting for three months for his visa application to be processed. "I see no border. No sign," he said in English. "Speak for peace and illegal. No good."

But officials of the Immigration and Naturalization Service say that Mr. Baluchi was too impatient to wait his turn for a visa and he jumped the border instead. And, officials say, since the Sept. 11, 2001, attacks, an Iranian camping in the desert raises a red flag.

So Mr. Baluchi waits in detention, running laps to keep in shape until a judge can decide whether to grant him asylum or deport him to Iran.

Mr. Baluchi has a lawyer, and she says she could probably arrange for bail of as little as $1,500. He would not even have to pay the bail himself because Arizona has a large number of Iranian immigrants and they have offered to give him the money and also give him a bed and a job. But he has cheerfully turned them down, expecting to be freed.

"I like free," Mr. Baluchi said sitting in the visitors' room in his prison blues, explaining that he will not accept bail because the quicker he sees the judge, the quicker his release. "I like to stay. I no go out." Three things are in his favor. It is said that Judge Freerks, the judge who will preside over his case, likes to hear a good story. Also, Mr. Baluchi is as sweet and enthusiastic as anyone can be. And he has a book of photographs and newspaper clippings from various countries to document his story.

"He's got this indomitable spirit," said Suzannah Maclay, Mr. Baluchi's lawyer who is representing him for free. "He sort of doesn't believe he's detained. And if he wins, he said he will run from California to New York."

The life of Reza Baluchi began in Rasht, in northern Iran near the Caspian Sea. The youngest of eight children, he watched as his brother returned from the war with Iraq a broken, brittle man. As he grew older, Mr. Baluchi drifted away from Islam, and when he was caught drinking during Ramadan, he was punished with a public beating. Later he was put in prison because he was accused of plotting against the government.

Asked for proof of his imprisonment, Mr. Baluchi pulled down his collar and showed a collarbone knotted in the shape of a horseshoe. He said he was beaten by prison guards.

When he was released, Mr. Baluchi says, he jumped on his Centurion bicycle and set out to see the world, to tell people what war did to his brother, and that war was no good. He was a refugee, but not like the other refugees who flee their countries. He was an adventurer, as opposed to the millions who walk to the neighboring border to spend their lives in a tent waiting for a handout of rice.

Mr. Baluchi is no more than 5 feet 6 inches and 150 pounds. He has small, expressive hands, large batlike ears, an odd tuft of hair on his forehead and—from all that bicycling—huge calves the size of pork roasts.

Along his journey, he has been snowed upon, soaked by slashing rains, sliced apart by the sun, attacked by insects, nearly done in by hunger. He went weeks without bathing and days without eating. In Congo, the army robbed him. He contracted malaria in South Africa and diarrhea in the Amazon. He was the victim of a hit-and-run accident in Mexico, and he could not figure the workings of chopsticks in China. He worked for a while as an auto mechanic in Portugal. Other times, when he had no money, strangers took him in. He shows photos of himself with minor bureaucrats in Africa and South America. One shows the Panamanian police escorting him to the Costa Rican border as the public waves him on. He developed no new philosophy, he said, just became more certain of what he believed at the start. Peace is good. War is bad.

Originally, he had planned to end his trip in Canada and not even try to enter the United States. But on Sept. 11, 2001, he was standing in the middle of Paris, when he heard about the attacks on the World Trade Center and the Pentagon. At that moment, he says, his final stop became clear. He would ride to Ground Zero and present to the American people the good wishes that he had collected on his travels. But he was caught. And now he may not get there. "I sorry," he said. "I make mistake. I love America."

"I go Ground Zero," he said. "I have something for people. Love."

Charlie LeDuff

She's His Oldest Friend

NEW YORK, N.Y.—Late in the afternoon, the old woman knew to look for him. Four o'clock. Their time.

The young man entered her tidy room in the nursing home, where the pillow on her bed is winsomely inscribed, "If things get better with age, then I'm approaching magnificence." Her roommate was out. After adjusting the cushion in her wheelchair, the young man steered the old woman down to the day room at the Jewish Home and Hospital nursing home on West 106th Street in Manhattan. She likes to sit there, for some variety in the slow ebb and flow of her life.

He read her mail for her: opera news, jokes her daughter had found on the Internet. She chuckled. She pressed him about whether he was exercising. "No, but I will," he said. "I'm going to swim." She said, "I always tell young people, live right, because in your old age it will tell on you."

Another resident sat down at the piano. She flailed away, unable to summon the right notes.

The old woman said, "My grandmother used to say, 'You spend a lifetime learning and then you forget it all.'" The young man said, "Maybe I should just skip some of the remembering."

Two people, the young man and the old woman, day after day. Elvis Checo is 20. Margaret Oliver is 93. A full 73 years of separation, yet when they are together time collapses. She makes him feel older. He makes her feel younger. Ms. Oliver says, "When we're together, it's like we're the same age." Many intergenerational connections are fleeting, lacking density. Once in a while, though, youth and age in juxtaposition build into something luminous and eternal. Something having to do with two people liking each other, no matter their ages.

When Elvis Checo was 15, he wanted something to fill the summer, and contacted the Department for the Aging's intergenerational office. He was referred to the Jewish Home and Hospital, and the volunteer office started him off wheeling people to recreational therapy, helping with the activities. Later, the home hired him to assist in the religious life department.

Nearly two years ago, a daughter of Ms. Oliver showed up in the volunteer office looking for someone to spend time with her mother. Elvis, barely 18, was willing. The daughter agreed to pay him $10 an hour, money to fill his empty pockets, if he would come to the Home for an hour every Tuesday, Wednesday and Thursday at 4.

At first, Ms. Oliver wondered, what would a teenager want with her—someone rolling around in a wheelchair, who relishes opera, who does not use a computer, who cannot even get the remote control to work? Elvis wondered, what would an old woman want with him—a spirited teenager still trying to decipher girls, who relaxes with video games and rap music, who likes to toss down a few beers with the guys?

Yet she felt the glow of Elvis. Those liquid eyes, that enchanting smile. Best of all, he did not treat her as some dithering fossil but as a friend. And Ms. Oliver was the flip side of what Elvis imagined. She did not look on him as a spacey drudge. She was fun. He could even tell her risqué jokes and she would laugh uproariously.

An odd balance formed. Another resident later hired Mr. Checo
to help with his physical therapy, and he finds himself in the home
every day. Pretty much daily, he bounces in to see Ms. Oliver. He
gets paid for just three hours but sees her far more often. He wants to.
She reminds him of his grandmother in the Dominican Republic.

And so evolved not "Tuesdays with Morrie" but Everyday with
Ms. Oliver.

Ms. Oliver has short steel-gray hair, empathic eyes. A former
dressmaker, originally from Augusta, Ga., both her husbands long
dead, she moved into the nursing home two years ago. Hobbled by
arthritis, she cannot walk much, knows this is the best place for her.
As in any nursing home, the accent is on filling the hours in an environment missing the high drama of life beyond its doors.

She watches TV—C-Span, the BBC, Court TV—but easily tires
of the passivity of television viewing. She reads, especially Agatha
Christie, listens to classical music and opera. There's Bingo, a trivia
game, lectures. Family members visit when they can: twin daughters,
who are 70, four grandchildren, three great-grandchildren. She goes
to bed at 9, is up at 7:30 and still has improbable amounts of time on
her hands.

The slow ticking of time is old age's exhaustive song, creating a
tension that never goes away. "Every now and then I say, 'Why am I
here?'" Ms. Oliver said. "My answer is this is the way of life and
nature made it this way. So you deal with it as much as possible by
distracting yourself. Otherwise you look around at the people who
are worse than you and you realize that could be you. Because you're
not going to get better. You're not going to get younger. When you
live in a nursing home, you lose anticipation. You're not anticipating
meeting someone or going somewhere or seeing something new.
That anticipation is a very big part of what's enjoyable about life.
There isn't much to look forward to at this age."

Elvis piped up, "Miss Oliver, think of it as you're having a little
vacation from everything you've done before."

She gave a good laugh. "Oh, Elvis," she said. "You're like a breath
of spring."

Seeing her so much, he understands her alternative universe.

"Reaching old age is loneliness, depression," he said. "You don't feel you're part of the world anymore. You're in the way. You're a pest. You have to depend on someone. That disturbs Miss Oliver. My goal is to make her still feel part of the world."

Mozart was on the radio. Ms. Oliver's eyes were closed when Elvis arrived. They went to the day room, got a choice spot. It has a wall of windows facing 106th Street, upholstered chairs, two enormous fish tanks, a piano. One of the residents, a jazz musician, likes to play the piano. He has lost both legs. He plays beautifully, but Ms. Oliver can always tell something is off, because he cannot press the pedals. "So you going to have a Chunky today?" Elvis asked. "What do you think?" Ms. Oliver said. "I've got my Bingo money. I've won three straight times."

Early on, Elvis discovered Ms. Oliver's weakness for ginger ale and Chunkys. So he routinely brings her the drink and the candy. Their private ritual.

He told her he was worried about a friend: "He's traveling around in the moon, as usual. He can't make up his mind on things." She said, "Remember what you learned from me about making decisions." He said, "Yes, learning how to say no."

"And then learning how to evaluate a situation and see if it changes," she said.

He said, "Yeah, I told you how my brother had his first kid when he was 15. He has three kids and he's 26. With three different women. He didn't learn. Now he's learning. The difference between him and me is he just lives the moment. I look five years ahead. I got that from you."

His eyes stared into hers.

No getting around it, Elvis has had a down-and-out life of hardship and forced maturity. Growing up in the Dominican Republic, poor, he drank water laced with sugar in place of juice. He recalls only one toy, a police car. Someone stole it. His father, a plumber, left when he was days old. His mother moved to New York, scratching out a living with a food truck, and he joined her when he was 9. His mother had her truck, serving cooked food out in the street. He helped, grilling burgers in the truck. He got out of school and cooked until 2 in the morning, got to bed at 3, got up three hours later for school.

Homework? Forget it.

When Elvis was 15, his mother returned for a while to the Dominican Republic, her wrists injured from the endless flipping of burgers. Elvis stayed in New York. Fifteen, living alone, supporting himself, just barely, from work at the nursing home. Sometimes he went two days without eating.

He still lives alone, in a forlorn room in Washington Heights, just a bed, a bureau, a TV and two chairs, a tiny kitchen he finds too foul and roach-ridden to use. "To go home, I have to go through five different drug stops," he said. "Those are the opportunities I see. That's the success I see. I've never done any of that. I've come here and seen there's another future, another life. It keeps me out of the street, out of trouble, and teaches me how to be a professional."

Ms. Oliver understands his complicated life and its weight, and has helped him clarify his purpose. He graduated from high school in February 2001, took a break, and plans to start at La Guardia Community College next month. He wants to go places. He intends to arrange his classes so he can still work at the nursing home and, of course, keep visiting Ms. Oliver.

He glanced over at her. "Miss Oliver makes me feel I am someone," he said. They were feasting on a Chunky. "Here's the last piece of Chunky," he said. "That's going to be my last Chunky," she said. He arched his eyebrows: "Oh yeah, who you kidding?"

Old people. Why do the young ignore them? Why do they make them invisible, irrelevant? Ms. Oliver wonders about these things. One day she said to Elvis: "My son-in-law said that Eskimos used to put the old people up with the walruses and they ate them and then they killed the walruses. There's a tribe in Africa I heard where after a certain age they put old people up in the hills and let them fend for themselves."

Elvis frowned. "We ought to look up to old people," he said. "They know so much. Look at you. I can't believe all you know."

She beamed at him. That Elvis, what a charmer. She once suggested he should go into the ministry, boy would he be perfect.

She also appreciates that there is plenty he knows that she does not. Once she asked him whether he was into rap music, an enigma to her, and he said, sure, he liked to rhyme with his friends, do some battles. She learned about CD's from him.

She wagged her head. "I'm still puzzled how they get messages up to outer space."

"Satellites, Miss Oliver," Elvis said.

They've gotten so close they feel they're plugged into each other's minds. Whenever Ms. Oliver needs help with something, Elvis seems to materialize. The other day, she wanted the tape flipped in her tape player, and her arthritic hands could not manage it. Sorcererlike, Elvis appeared. Aides hector them about the time they spend together: "What, are you two an item?" Ms. Oliver laughs and says: "I'm almost 75 years older than Elvis. Some item!"

The dinner hour. He slid her into her assigned seat. On the wall beside her was a board that gave the day, the date, the next holiday, the season, the weather—the latest particulars at a timeless place. They clucked about Birthday Girl. It was their code name for one of the aides, lets them camouflage their gossip. The gossip tumbled out. Mr. Checo said a secretary had been flirting with him. What to do? She said: "Ask her if she'd like to see 'Chicago.' And you know what she'll say: 'I thought you'd never ask.'"

As usual, Elvis filled out her weekly menu, and they went through the options: tuna sandwich or veal, cheese ravioli or breaded fish. He knows her tastes so well he really does not need to ask—always takes the hot dog and beans, cranberry juice, ice cream every day.

After dinner, back in the day room. They resumed their easy chitchat, the back and forth of their simple declarative sentences. They talked about going to a pizza parlor when the weather improved—a modest excursion that meant anticipation, possibility. Ms. Oliver's face shone.

Then Elvis turned serious: "A friend of mine recently got shot right in the neck. He's alive, he's O.K., but he was on the ground, twitching, and it was hard seeing that, someone you're friends with."

"What was it?" Ms. Oliver said.

"It was a stray bullet," he said.

She gave a worried look. "You have to watch yourself, Elvis," she said. "Soon, I hope, you'll get out of there."

Mr. Checo said that after college he might apply to medical school. "The question is if I get the scholarship," he said.

"You would make a great doctor," she said. "You know, Elvis, it's important to lead your life in a meaningful way. So you don't get old and say I should have done this and I should have done that. I don't feel that way." Elvis said, "I have those same thoughts, but you put it into words."

"The thing is, don't beat yourself up," Ms. Oliver said.

"I used to be really hard on myself, because I felt I had to prove something," Elvis said. "I grew up being what a psychiatrist would call an obsessive-compulsive person. Then I came here and I met you and I saw you laugh about things and I calmed down. I take things easier because I see you do."

"You know something, Elvis, I don't feel old," she said.

Elvis said, "You don't seem old to me."

The room began emptying out, the low throb of voices evaporating. They gazed out the windows of this place for the old. Storm clouds threatened in the packed gray sky. Spring on 106th Street. Ms. Oliver asked him to drape her blanket over her legs. "My legs get cold," she said. "When I was young I would see people sitting like this with blankets over their legs and I didn't know why. It's because your knees get cold."

She said that she had just had her monthly weighing and had gained two pounds since last month: "It's all that chocolate."

"You've got to watch your figure, huh?" Elvis said. He gave her an impish smile. He asked her, "Want to have a Chunky?"

Ms. Oliver smiled back. "Why Elvis, I thought you'd never ask."

N. R. Kleinfield

It Takes a Village to Turn a Farmer into a Lawyer

MONKTON, Vt.—The classified advertisement was tucked away on page 22 of the *Addison County Independent* newspaper: "Heartfelt thanks," it began, "to all the friends and neighbors who supported our family during the three long years Sam was in Boston at school. You chauffeured the kids, helped Eugenie fix things, chase heifers, and keep a sense of humor."

The ad went on to make special mention of the teachers at the Monkton Central School, "who showed us enthusiasm for lifelong learning." Even, it added, "in a middle-aged farmer's Quixotic journey to law school."

"We survived," the ad said. "Sam's home."

Eugenie Doyle, a 46-year-old substitute teacher at the elementary school, spent $19.60 to place that ad. She wanted it to be seen by the 1,687 people who live in this tiny farming community, which is about 55 miles south of the Canadian border. These friends and neighbors had stepped in when her husband couldn't, and she wanted them to know how much they had helped.

"When you say thank you," she said in an interview, "you realize how much you've been given, and how rich you are."

Ms. Doyle's husband, Sam Burr, had been a dairy farmer for 20 years. It was the only job he ever knew, or ever wanted, but it is not an easy line of work. In the past decade, milk prices started falling and Mr. Burr had run up losses of $30,000. So, at the age of 44, he decided to go to become a lawyer. He picked the law, he said, because he "wanted to make a difference." There were 3,688 dairy farmers in Vermont when he bought his first farm in 1975; twenty years later there were 1,770. And those who were left, Mr. Burr reasoned, could probably use an advocate who understood the problems they faced.

Mr. Burr picked Northeastern University in Boston, 260 miles southeast, because it was close enough for him to travel home on the weekends. It was also far enough away, he admits, that he could escape for a while. Two years earlier, he had been forced to auction the last of the 59 heifers in his herd. And for a man who prefers the company of cows to people—his cows' names, including Rocket and Lulu, are memorialized in a folder on his desk titled "Gone But Not Forgotten"—there was only so much empty barn he could take.

"There is nothing more frustrating than being on a farm, watching things go downhill and not being able to figure out how not to make it happen," he said, walking past rows of organic strawberries grown by his wife to provide "grocery money" in his absence.

Holding out hope that they could find him something else to do, his wife had begged him not to go to law school. "It seemed like, first the cows go, then the equipment, then the farmer," she said. But he scraped together the tuition by selling land and taking loans from relatives, and off to Boston he went.

It would not be his first time in school there: Mr. Burr had graduated from Harvard in 1974 with a degree in anthropology. This time, at Northeastern, he discovered that he loved learning about the law and became an active participant in class discussions, where fellow students referred to him as Pops. Meanwhile, his wife and family missed him. On the first day of school after he had left, Ms. Doyle got a flat tire with three of her children in the car. She realized she would have to call a neighbor for help, but that was hardly something that came naturally.

"Farmers can be really isolated," she said. "You kind of stick to yourselves."

She did call, and John Padua, who owns a nearby nursery, responded. Ms. Doyle wanted to fix the tire herself. He took the kids to school.

Other acts of kindness followed, and Ms. Doyle started to keep a log of them so she wouldn't forget who to thank: someone fixed the furnace in the middle of the night, someone else moved the refrigerator, and any number picked up one child at soccer practice while she picked up the other. When a bull broke free from the yard, a neighbor managed to catch it by the horns, and, twisting it by the tail, led it home. Now Mr. Burr, too, has come home, and his family is getting used to the idea of seeing him in a suit. Before this year, he had only owned two: a black one from high school, which still fit, and one he inherited from his grandfather two decades ago.

He is working, for the time being, at the Vermont Legislative Council, a government agency that helps legislators draft bills. Though he still hopes to use the law to help farmers, he has not quite figured out how.

For now, Mr. Burr works in a cramped office next to the Statehouse, where atop his computer sits a faded blue corduroy hat, with the name of the Blue Seal grain company emblazoned on the front. He had worn it, he said, every day of his life as a farmer.

Jacques Steinberg

MUSIC UNDERGROUND

NEW YORK, N.Y.—The experts say that 12-year-old David Allakhverdov is not quite ready to play his piano at Carnegie Hall. But the commuters racing for their subways underneath Times Square seem to disagree.

They thought the little boy with the gentle features and mane of dark hair was a miraculous talent, a genius, "a little Mozart," as one woman was heard to whisper to herself as she walked through the train station where David was playing his electric piano keyboard.

Actually, the playing was not perfect, but it was amazing and inspiring. Once in a while the notes rang so true and clear that the talent at the keyboard was unmistakable. And, after all, the boy was only 12.

It has just been a year since David came to New York with his family from Tashkent, Uzbekistan. His family is Armenian, and felt increasingly threatened by the Uzbek majority there. David once had stones thrown at him on the streets of Tashkent. His parents were both doctors back there, but here they can only work in low-paying jobs while they prepare for exams that will allow them to practice medicine again. Meanwhile, the family of five is crowded into the lower half of a two-family home.

David, who "sang before he talked," his mother said, and who attended a special music school since he was very young, also had to interrupt his "career." "When we came, nobody knew David, we knew no teachers, no nothing," Mrs. Allakhverdov said.

But the family began to notice that musicians would stand and play in the subways and that passers-by would listen. "That's how we decided to go to the subway," Mrs. Allakhverdov said. "There are many people there, and many good musicians. We thought maybe it was the American style." They first tried the Columbus Circle station, but found it too noisy, she said. "A friend told us to try Times Square."

So now David, who still speaks very little English, goes down into the subways once or twice a week with the electric piano his parents bought just for this purpose. Sometimes he is accompanied by his 18-year-old brother Arthur, and sometimes his parents come along. David, a seventh grader in a public junior high school that does not offer music classes, said he is happiest when he is playing, and to watch him is to see how true that is.

Mr. and Mrs. Allakhverdov said they were surprised when people began dropping dollar bills in front of David's piano. They are not surprised anymore, of course—David has a business card now, and he keeps the money he earns. It helped buy the used upright piano that stands in the family living room. In October, he played at the wedding of David Udell and Alice Blank; Mr. Udell, a lawyer, had heard him during his daily commute.

"I liked the idea of it," Mr. Udell said. "We're a New York couple, and it was a New York wedding, and his seemed like such a New York story."

And how did David do? "He was spellbinding," Mr. Udell said.

Other things have happened since he began playing underground. He started studying with a professor at the Juilliard School of Music. He auditioned for the conductor of the Hartford Symphony in Connecticut. The conductor was so impressed he called David's teacher and asked if the boy could appear as a soloist with the symphony. The teacher advised against it, saying that he had more studying to do before he reached his full potential.

The teacher, Seymour Lipkin, is not charging David for his weekly lessons. He said his goal was to prepare David for a spring audition for the very prestigious full-time program at Juilliard. "There's a big talent in there, but he's in a primitive state," Mr. Lipkin said. "He's a boy who has learned a lot of stuff by himself. What he needs now is to sit for six or seven years and to be trained to be an artist. It's clear he's very gifted; he really wants to tell you something and you really want to listen to him. It just pours out of him."

And so it does. During a visit to the family's home, David was very quiet. He answered the questions put to him in brief phrases. Yes, he does read music. He does not know how many pieces he has memorized but he can play without repeating a piece for two and a half hours. What does he think about as he plays? "How to make the music," he said, a little impatiently. It was evident he wanted to be asked to play; when he was, he leaped at the chance. And as he touched the keys, his whole demeanor changed. He pursed his lips, and his eyes became fiery. Tossing his hair, he banged on a chord and lifted his hand with a dramatic flourish. When he was finished, the Chopin nocturne lingered in the room in tinny echo. The visitors applauded. Nobody said anything.

Bruce Weber

Years passed. Another reporter, Randy Kennedy, visited David to see where life had led him. Here's what he wrote:

Some things have not changed in five years. David is 17 now, but he still doesn't have a tuxedo. (He gets by with a bow tie and a dark suit.) He still doesn't have a good piano at home in the Bronx. ("The good ones, $30,000, at least!" says his father, Vitaliy.)

He still has an astounding amount of hair for someone his size.

("In classical music," David explains, his English still a little choppy, "you should have lot of hair. It make you look like a star.")

Most important, David still does what first brought him to this newspaper's attention: once a week, he lugs an electric piano into the subway, puts fingers to keys and instantly makes crowds of sour-faced subway riders stop and smile, almost against their will, as if hundred-dollar bills were being handed out. But in the years since his last interview, David Allakhverdov has managed to find an accompaniment more fitting than the clack of the No. 2 train: a 65-piece orchestra.

First, a little recent history. With the help of his teacher, the concert pianist Seymour Lipkin, David auditioned four years ago for the highly competitive pre-college program at Juilliard.

He did not make the cut.

But the disappointment, Mr. Lipkin recalled, only seemed to draw out of David the kind of determination that may one day make him a great pianist. "He just dug his heels in," Mr. Lipkin said. "He worked hard for a year, and then he made it."

A year after he got in on his second try, David won an honors recital competition, and the prize was a $5,000 scholarship. Soon he didn't have as much time to play in the subways, because he started accepting invitations to play in concerts.

Then last month, he beat out 10 other young Juilliard finalists for a spot as the soloist with a youth symphony. It was the first time he had played with a full orchestra.

David and his family still live in the same crowded half of a two-family house. But things are slowly turning around. Mrs. Allakhverdov recently passed her state exams and will begin working at Interfaith Medical Center as a resident in internal medicine.

David's brother, Arthur, 22, will begin medical school in the fall. His sister, Christine, 21, is finishing a nursing program, and his father devotes most of his time to managing David's blossoming career. Then there is David, who could not be happier, despite the fact that he still has no girlfriend. ("I guess the piano, she is my girlfriend," he says, slouching even more than usual and rolling his eyes.)

Last Friday, at the last rehearsal before the symphony concert,

David waited nervously for the Steinway grand to be rolled into place. Instead of fanning tux tails over the bench, he just yanked his long blue T-shirt down over his jeans and eased his white Nikes onto the pedals.

When David finished the dramatic last movement—a head-snapping, hair-tossing performance—the symphony's conductor waited for silence to fill the room and then simply pointed with the baton at the skinny young pianist.

At Juilliard, the tradition is for students to applaud by stomping their feet. For a few seconds that evening, it sounded like a stampede.

ENDING THE SILENCE

VALHALLA, N.Y.—The last sounds that Hermine Wilber ever heard were the bombs being dropped on the city of Vienna. That was more than 50 years ago, during World War II, when she was only 15 years old. Mrs. Wilber lived in Austria then, a country that had been taken over by the Nazi army during the war. Her father was an Austrian who thought the Nazis were evil, and when he spoke his thoughts aloud his children were expelled from school and the family was forced to hide from the soldiers.

One night all those years ago, Mrs. Wilber began to feel very sick. Her head throbbed and ached and she was hot to the touch with a fever. Her parents could not take her to a hospital, for fear they would all be discovered by the Nazis, so they took her to a nearby shelter instead, where there was no medicine. For two weeks she was sick, and when she finally recovered she could not hear at all.

Mrs. Wilber was sad that she couldn't hear, but was happy to be alive, and by the time the war ended she had learned to read people's lips. Vienna was filled with American soldiers, who had driven out the Nazis, and one night she met one of those soldiers, a man named Bill Wilber. They began dating, and for months Mr. Wilber did not know that this cheerful, animated young woman, with beautiful bright red hair, was deaf—because she read lips so well.

Bill and Hermine were married and they moved back to America, to Mr. Wilber's farm. Mrs. Wilber learned to read lips in English—a language she had rarely ever heard—and to raise a family. Mr. Wilber's job included work during the night, so Mrs. Wilber kept their children in bed with her so she could see and feel their cries. When the children were in school she loved to paint and write poetry, and several of her poems were published in poetry books. She also loved to dance even though she could not hear the music. Instead she sensed the vibrations, counted the beats in her head, and watched the other dancers. "The music was still in my heart," she said.

She missed not being able to hear. Every day she went for a walk near the farm, and although she could gaze at the mountains, she could never hear the birds or the waterfalls. She wanted to know what Elvis sounded like, and, most of all, to hear the laughter of her children.

One day, more than 50 years after she first became deaf, Mrs. Wilber learned about an operation called cochlear implant surgery. It can make some deaf people hear again. During the operation, which takes three hours and costs $40,000, surgeons insert a tiny machine in the ear—a man-made replacement for the nerves which had been broken by her illness.

First doctors implant this gumball-sized device. Then, a month later, they turn it on. For that breathtaking moment, Mrs. Wilber gathered her whole family at the doctor's office. Fourteen of her relatives were in the tiny room, including her husband, her brother, her sister, three of her children, five grandchildren and two great grandchildren.

"Are you ready?" asked the technician, named Sara Morton, who specializes in cochlear implants.

"Am I ready?" answered Mrs. Wilber, after reading Ms. Morton's lips, "55 years."

Then Ms. Morton held a piece of paper in front of her mouth so that Mrs. Wilber could not see what her lips were doing. "Bop, bop, bop," Ms. Morton said.

Right away, Mrs. Wilber repeated the sounds she had just *heard*. "Bop, bop, bop."

Everyone around her, all these people who loved her, started to cry. "Come on," Mrs. Wilber said with a happy smile. "Talk to me."

Her oldest daughter, also named Hermine, put her hand gently over her mother's eyes and said words Mrs. Wilber had never heard before: "I love you, Mom."

Her grandson, Thomas, who is a teenager, tried to speak, but he was crying too hard with happiness to get any words out.

Her husband, Bill, walked up to her and said, softly, "I met you in 1946." It was the first time she had ever heard his voice. He asked her if he sounded as she had imagined. Yes, she said, his voice was low and strong.

From every corner of her world there was sound. The hum of the air-conditioner. The lawn mower outside the window. Her own voice on a recording she'd made back in Vienna in 1944. What, she wondered, was that strange clacking noise? Her heels on the wooden floor. And that high-pitched squeal, one that surely didn't exist when she was a girl? That was her granddaughter's pager, which made Mrs. Wilber jump as it welcomed her back to the world of sound.

Corey Kilgannon

LIFE IN AN AIRPORT

ROISSY, France—He has received hundreds of letters of encouragement, many of them addressed only to "Sir Alfred, Charles de Gaulle Airport." And even though that is not a real address, the letters were delivered. Everyone at the airport post office knew just where he was, sitting quietly on a red plastic bench on the lower level of Terminal 1, his belongings stacked neatly on a luggage cart.

"Sir Alfred," whose real name is Merhan Karimi Nasseri, is an Iranian exile who has lived at the passenger area of this airport near Paris for more than 10 years. At first he stayed because he did not have a passport and was not permitted to leave. Then he stayed because he had spent so much time in the airport that he was afraid of life outside.

"He is scared to leave this bubble world he has been living in," said Dr. Philippe Bargain, the airport's medical director. "Finally getting the papers has been a huge shock to him, as if he was just thrown from his horse. When you wait 11 years for something and suddenly in a few minutes you sign some papers and it's done—imagine what a shock that is."

Mr. Nasseri, a thin, stooped man with sad eyes, seems uncomfortable with the question of what he will do next. One day he announced that he would be going to Finland, only to change his mind within 24 hours. He says he must consider his future carefully. He may want to go to Belgium or England. But his eyes really light up when he talks about the airport.

People who race through to catch a plane do not notice what a nice place it can be to live, he says. It has everything he seems to need. His "home" is a spot between the pizzeria and an electronics store, and his days are punctuated by the rhythm of the flights. Bustling travelers gather in the morning and dwindle away in the evening. Tidy and dignified, Mr. Nasseri remains on his bench. He shaves with an electric razor every morning, washes up in the passenger rest room and takes his clothes to the cleaner here.

He has survived for years on the kindness of strangers. He never begs. But airport employees routinely give him their meal coupons. Flight attendants give him toiletries left over from the first-class passengers. Occasionally, people who have heard his story send him money in the mail. One traveler gave him a sleeping bag and a camping mattress, though he generally prefers to sleep on his curved bench.

"The airport is not bad," Mr. Nasseri said. "It is very active and functions every day. I see different passengers every week from all over the world and it is quite interesting."

Mr. Nasseri arrived at the airport with a one-way ticket to London, a few clothes, about $500 and no passport. He told airport authorities that his papers had been stolen at a Paris train station. Waiving the usual rules, the authorities let him fly to Heathrow airport in London.

But there, British immigration officials refused to let him enter the country, and he was returned to Charles de Gaulle, here in France. Except for the occasional trip to a lawyer's office, he has not left since.

French authorities say they would gladly help him go home, but it is unclear exactly where that might be. He seems confused about that subject, and it is possible he has lost his memory, because he sometimes tells one story and sometimes another. Dr. Bargain says it has been confirmed that Mr. Nasseri was born in Iran, in the town of Masjid-i-Sulaiman, in 1945. The doctor says it is also likely that, as Mr. Nasseri says, his father was a physician. But what happened to him between 1945 and 1988, the year he arrived at the airport, is less clear.

What he found particularly odd, Dr. Bargain said, was that, even with all the articles and television reports done on Mr. Nasseri over the years, no one had ever contacted the airport, saying they knew him.

"You would have thought that there was someone out there, a family member, someone he went to school with, someone who knew him in London, someone who would have come forward and said, 'I know this man.' But it never happened. It was like a big void."

Mr. Nasseri has told various officials that his family sent him to study in Britain, and court papers show that he was there in the mid-1970's. Mr. Nasseri has said that while he was in Britain his family stopped sending him money. He came back to Iran to ask them why, he has said, and while he was home he was arrested by police who said he had participated in antigovernment protests while in Britain. His family managed to get him released from jail, he said, but the government shipped him out of the country immediately on a passport that only lasted a year and could not be renewed.

No one knows what he did for years after that. In 1986, he has said, he was granted asylum by the government of Belgium, but he lost those papers in a Paris train station in 1988. That was when he came to the Paris airport, he says, hoping to take a plane to England because his mother was British. Authorities tried to confirm parts of his story, with no success.

So he has lived in the airport, and, over the years, he has become a small celebrity here. French television has done a documentary on him. When news leaked out that he would be leaving, half a dozen international journalists appeared for the occasion. Mr. Nasseri clearly enjoys the attention.

He is now allowed to leave because a human rights lawyer finally got the government of Belgium to hand over papers proving that he really was a political refugee. Once they had those documents, the French government could grant him a new set of papers—ones which allow him to leave the airport.

Mr. Nasseri has tried to keep track of the outside world during his years in the airport. He listens to the news for hours each day, meticulously recording much of what he hears in a diary that now takes up seven cardboard boxes. He considers the breakup of the Soviet Union the most important single event.

For a while, he said, he took a correspondence course in business administration. But he no longer does that. He does like reading, however, and has more than 50 books tucked away on a trolley.

Most of the airport workers here call him "Alfred," though no one can remember how the nickname started. Most say they can understand how it would be hard for him to leave.

"Really, even if he has the papers, where does he go?" said Sergio Parreira, manager of the McDonald's on the lower level. "The world is a little savage outside these walls. He has been protected all this time. And at his age, how do you start over?"

Dr. Bargain said the airport took no action against Mr. Nasseri because there was nowhere to send him. But now that he has his papers they would contact social agencies to help him make the move.

"He will have to be weaned from the airport, like an addict really," Dr. Bargain said. "Still, it does make you wonder what kind of a society we live in that this can happen to a man."

Suzanne Daley

Two Sisters and Their Cows

MUD CITY, Vt.—Today was the day they auctioned the Lepine sisters' 129 prized cows. Gertrude, who is 68, Jeannette, who is 66, and Therese, who is 71—are known throughout Vermont, and beyond. So are the Jersey cows they have been milking, feeding and cleaning up after for more than four decades.

"They've got the best herd in the state," said Howard Morse, a 79-year-old milk salesman, who has known the Lepine (pronounced Leh-PEEN) sisters since they were small. "Everyone knows that."

His voice displayed awe. A lot of men around here sound awed when they talk about the Lepine sisters, and their cows. One auctioneer, Neal Smith, told the sisters it was an honor for him to sell their cows. Farmers from all over the state drove up to the sisters' farm in Mud City, a bend in the road north of Stowe, for the privilege of bidding on one of the cows, while others phoned in bids from Idaho, New York, Oklahoma, Utah and Wisconsin. Mr. Morse joined the standing-room-only crowd under the big red-and-white tent out of respect for the Lepine sisters and because it seemed as though an era was ending.

One neighbor sent a basket of marigolds and daisies, with a note, "We won't call it retirement." Gert, as the middle sister is known to all, hung the basket on the rail around the auction pen. Several of the cows stopped to sniff the flowers as they took their turn through the sawdust.

The sisters are not selling the land where they grew up and where their father farmed before them, and they plan to stay right where they are, surrounded by the Green Mountains. But today's auction meant that Vermont will have one less dairy farm. When Gert decided she hated being a teacher and returned to the farm in 1952—Jeannette and Therese followed later—the state had more than 11,000 dairy farms. Today there are fewer than 1,200.

Gert recalled the day she realized, in the midst of teaching a class, that she would rather be milking cows. "I looked out the window and I said to myself, 'I'm out of here.' I wanted to be where I could sing when I wanted to and swear when I wanted to."

She lost $13,000 last year, she said. But she said that she was never in it for the money and that the real reason they are selling is Jeannette's bad knee. Jeannette, a former stewardess at Pan Am, took a bad fall while skiing in Austria about 40 years ago. She had a knee operation in December, and she was hobbling around the barn today, feeding the cows and toting milk pails. But she has not been able to help the way she used to. With Therese in failing health, that left Gert with more work than she could handle.

Around here, even the sisters' hands are famous. "Just look at their hands," Mr. Morse said. "They're rough and gnarled. That's manual labor that caused that."

Gert, a wiry woman in blue jeans, laughed, and held out her bruised left hand. "Sparkle stepped on it," she said. Sparkle is one of her cows.

Gert talked about each cow by name. "Here's Typhoon," she said, petting the cows that had not yet been loaded into trailers. "And here's Lizzie. Mighty Mite. Lynette. Goldie."

Then she came to Veronica, the star of the auction. "She went for $5,000," Gert said. "She's heading off to Utah. She comes from a great family."

During the auction, each cow, with a number stamped in indelible ink on her brown rump, took a turn in the ring, while Mr. Smith gushed over them: "Lot No. 12. Now we're going to sell the factory: 140,000 pounds of milk lifetime production and still looking this good after delivering a calf yesterday."

Therese cried when the auction began. Not so Jeannette and Gert. "It had to happen," Gert said.

No one ever gave her much trouble about being a female dairy farmer, she said, except once when a fertilizer salesman said to her, "You should be ashamed, that's a man's job." She said she asked him, "Who decides what's a man's job or a woman's job?"

Recalling the incident, she said, "I wasn't a farmer's wife, I was the farmer. The farmer's wife was doing the same thing, just like my mother, she worked beside my dad, only they called her the farmer's wife."

The sisters have rented their land to a young farming couple from Vermont. The sisters' labor is included. The sisters will also be busy with their art gallery a few miles away, where they display the work of local artists. Gert also hopes to get in some trout fishing. She has not been in 30 years. "Every day was a work day," she said. "I loved it."

Sara Rimer

The reporter, Sara Rimer, visited the sisters five years after they sold their cows. This is what she found:

MORRISVILLE, Vt.—Now that she no longer has to get up at 3:30 A.M. to milk the cows, Gert Lepine likes to lounge in bed until 6, reading the books she never had time for when she was farming. She has discovered Cormac McCarthy and reread much of Steinbeck and Hemingway. She has read Willa Cather's *My Ántonia* twice.

These August mornings, Gert has been deep in F. Scott Fitzgerald's *Tender Is the Night*. She turns 74 next month. She lives with her sisters Therese, 76, and Jeannette, 71, in the same farmhouse, on Mud City Loop, a bend of the road north of Stowe, where she has lived since she was 14.

The sisters dote on their beagle, Waldo, and their cats, Si and Tweeter, but when it comes to the Jersey cows that were once the pride of Vermont, they are no more sentimental than they are over the men they didn't marry.

"I had some great cows," Gert said. "I like to think back on them. But I don't miss them."

For nearly half a century, she took care of those cows. She also did the work on the farm, haying, fencing, clearing fields, chopping wood. At night, Gert recalled, she would be so exhausted, "I'd read a newspaper and fall asleep."

"I didn't have a day off in 45 years," Gert said. Now, she said, "every day is a new experience."

Now she has time for trout fishing, kayaking, hiking and going to auctions and art galleries. She and Jeannette run an art gallery in town, and the walls of the farmhouse are covered with paintings by the local artists they have befriended.

Jeannette also helps out with a community garden, and operates a maple sugaring business with a neighbor. Sometimes the sisters just jump in the car and drive. After all those years tied to the cows, much of her own state is new to Gert.

"I love just seeing Vermont," she said. "I've seen the Connecticut River for the first time in my life."

Talking at their dining room table on Saturday afternoon, Gert and Jeannette gave a matter-of-fact accounting of the years without cows while Therese sat quietly in a wheelchair, watching tennis on television. Therese, her sisters explained, had suffered a couple of bad strokes. They had put a hospital bed in the living room so they could keep her at home. They wouldn't dream of putting Therese in a nursing home, the sisters said.

Jeannette lost the vision in her left eye in a freak accident on a kayaking trip with Gert, but "I get around fine with the other eye," she said. The accident has not dimmed the sisters' enthusiasm for kayaking.

"We just got a new kayak," Gert said. "We were out on Shelburne Pond yesterday. There was wildlife like I've never seen."

Four years ago, their barn burned to the ground. The sisters rebuilt it, and now they have a new tenant farmer, who has his own herd of Jersey cows. The sisters like seeing the cows—and drinking the milk, straight from the tank in the barn. They have never seen any reason to switch to lowfat, and among them there is not the slightest sign of osteoporosis.

They may not have married, or had children, but still the Lepine sisters have led lives of commitment. "You're committed to the land," Gert said.

She and Jeannette gave a driving tour of their land, nearly 1,000 acres with stunning mountain views. Developers have offered them millions, but the sisters have turned the development rights over to the Vermont Land Trust, ensuring that the land will be preserved.

"I figure I've gone through 1,000 cows in my life," Gert said. "Cows you figure won't be with you always. But the land becomes so familiar to you. You know where every stone is."

Getting out of the car in the middle of a field, Jeannette pointed out one large stone. "How well I remember this stone," she said. "I'd say, 'Where is that bloody stone so it doesn't clobber my machinery.'"

She was hobbling on her bad knee, and looking around through her one good eye. Her sister was at her side. "Aren't we lucky?" Jeannette said.

ANIMALS

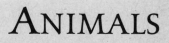

IT CAME. IT CLUCKED. IT CONQUERED

A true story about a chicken that showed up in the backyard of a New York Times *reporter.*

ASTORIA, Queens—One day in the dead of winter, I looked out my back window and saw a chicken. It was jet black with a crimson wattle, and it seemed unaware that it was in New York City. In classic barnyard fashion, it was scratching and pecking and clucking.

I looked closer, blinked a few times and shrugged. Birds come and go. Usually they're pigeons, not chickens, but like other birds, this one had wings and would probably use them. Or so I thought. Two months later it's still there. Not only is it still there, but I'm also feeding it, and it's feeding me, at the rate of five eggs a week. I have made the transition from homeowner to farmer, from food consumer to food producer. All because of one mysterious chicken that came and wouldn't leave.

The protagonist of this story has no name. It is known simply as the Chicken, a nonname that seems right, considering its obscure origins. How it came to a small backyard in Astoria, Queens, remains an unanswered question. The chicken made its first appearance next door, at the home of a family of cab drivers from Bangladesh. My wife, Nancy, and I decided that they must have bought the chicken and were fattening it for a feast. That theory changed when the chicken hopped the fence and began roaming around our yard. It began pacing the perimeter of the yard with a proprietary air, sizing things up with a shiny, appraising eye that said, I've seen better, but I've seen worse.

We now had a chicken. Very nice. But what next?

Eating it was out of the question. As a restaurant critic and an animal lover, I subscribe to a policy of complete hypocrisy. Serve me fish or meat in any form, but don't ask me to watch the killing. Once I meet it, I don't want to eat it. Besides, Nancy and I had come up with another origin theory that roused our protective instincts. The chicken, we concluded, had escaped from a live poultry market about four blocks away. It was on the run.

Our hearts went out to the brave little refugee. Returning it to the market would be tantamount to murder. Eat it? Never. We had to save it.

Both of us suddenly realized, however, that we knew quite a bit about the consumption side of the chicken equation, and absolutely nothing about the production side. We didn't yet know whether our chicken was male or female, for one thing. It didn't crow in the morning, and it didn't have a comb, so female seemed a safe bet. But then again, neither of us had ever had to answer the question. There were other questions, too. Would the chicken freeze to death out there? What do chickens eat? Do they have to live in a coop? Do chickens get lonely without other chickens? Do they need roosters to lay eggs? As I racked my brain for chicken knowledge, about the only thing I dredged up was a piece of trivia: they are easy to hypnotize. I knew this because Al Gore often recalled happy days in Tennessee when he would line up chickens on a porch and put them into a trance.

A colleague put me in touch with a real-life farmer, Steve Townley of Milford, N.J. He calmed me down. "Chickens will eat just about anything," he said. "They'll eat vegetables. They'll even eat grass." Cold, it seemed, would not kill my chicken off. "They just fluff their feathers," Mr. Townley said. A chicken coop, it turns out, is aimed at protecting the birds from predators. If there are no predators, there's really no need for a coop.

Chickens were beginning to sound like the ideal pet. Not a lot of personality, but undemanding. Why doesn't everyone in New York have one?

The chicken took to its new surroundings easily. Its main social task was to make friends with the local cat society, a core group of about five strays that we feed. Two of them, enormous gray tomcat brothers called Bruiser and Crusher have a strong sense of territory, although they do allow a B-team of lesser cats to drop by for a meal. How would the two species deal with each other?

One morning, I looked out the window and saw four cats lined up at their food bowls and, right in the middle, eating with gusto, the chicken. Occasionally, it would push a cat aside to get a better position. Dry cat food from Costco suited it just fine.

The cats, for their part, regarded the chicken warily. To the extent that it was a bird, it was prey. But big prey. From time to time, they would stalk, press their bodies to the ground, swish their tails and give every sign of going for the kill. Then they would register the chicken's size and become gripped by second thoughts. A face-saving, half-hearted lunge would follow.

The two sides have reached parity. Sometimes I'll look out back and see a cat chasing the chicken. Ten minutes later, I'll see the chicken chasing a cat. When the chicken gets too pushy around the food, Bruiser or Crusher might swat it on the side of the head. I like to think they have reached the plane of mutual respect. Perhaps affection.

One day, I saw the chicken down on the ground, writhing and twisting and jerking in the dirt. Four cats encircled it, motionless, their faces a study in mingled horror and concern. This was it, I decided. The chicken was suffering from a chicken-like nerve disease and was dying in my yard. I couldn't bear to watch. Half an hour later, it was fine. It had been taking a dust bath.

The chicken showed real character the night that terror descended from the sky. It had already proved itself indifferent to bitter cold and heavy snow. But then it displayed bravery. A police helicopter, searchlight blazing, descended over my backyard, searching house to house for something or someone. I never did find out what or who.

But the helicopter hovered, and the downdraft from the blades set our pine tree swaying, turned over a wooden bench, flipped the cat igloo upside down and smashed heavy ceramic cat bowls. The chicken sleeps in the pine tree. I couldn't begin to imagine what was going through its tiny mind.

The next morning, amid wreckage out of *Apocalypse Now*, the chicken reappeared, brimful of vim and vigor. I looked at it with new respect. It looked at me the way it always does, with a grudgingly tolerant expression. In the bird's-eye view of things, I am the useful idiot who brings food. Actually, it took a while to sort out the food. It was nice to know that the chicken could eat anything, but cat food didn't seem right. The bird expert at one PetCo recommended wild-bird seed. The expert at another branch said, "We have birdseed for specific kinds of bird, but because the chicken is not a specific bird, we don't have any specific food." That stopped me cold. It's specifically a chicken, I wanted to say. I ended up buying a bag of parrot food. Finally, I did what any mature, thinking adult male would do in a crisis. I called my mother.

It was the right call. Mom flew into action. She drove to the local feed store in La Porte, Tex., and picked up a 25-pound bag of Cargill Scratch Grains, a blend of milo, corn and oats. She began shipping the grain in installments. The chicken, although still keen on cat food, seemed to appreciate the chicken feed, and I certainly preferred seeing it eat grain, especially after the grisly evening when I set out a treat for the cats—leftover shreds of chicken from a stockpot—and saw the chicken happily join in.

It seems to like variety and resists direction. My impression, from farmers in movies, was that chickens come running when you scatter the feed. This one runs when the cat food hits the bowls, but it looks on chicken feed as a between-meals snack. In any case, it prefers to wander throughout the day, digging here, pecking there and only occasionally stumbling on clusters of feed.

Our care paid off. One morning, Nancy spied a round object on the patio. An egg. Her eye followed the probable path of the egg and saw a cozy nest at the base of the pine tree. In the nest were four more eggs. They were small, with a color somewhere between ecru and beige, but this was it, the blessed event. Along with the herbs, the tomatoes and the zucchini, we could look forward to an endless supply of fresh eggs.

But how did they taste? We decided to put our eggs to the test against two top-rated organic free-range eggs, Horizon Organic, produced by Glenwood Farms in Jeterville, Va., and Knoll Krest Farm in Clinton Corners, N.Y.

Horizon (motto: "A Clean-Living Chicken Makes Real Good Eggs!") uses no antibiotics, pesticides or hormones, and its chickens live in "a healthy cage-free, free-roaming environment."

Knoll Krest, similarly, boasts that its chickens are fed natural ingredients without antibiotics or hormones, and that, further, the eggs are hand-gathered from "free running" hens. Does this mean that the Knoll Krest chickens are more energetic than Horizon's? When does roaming accelerate into running? In any case, my eggs certainly qualified as organic, and my chicken both roams and runs. The Horizon eggs were dark brown with a pale yellow yolk. The Knoll Krest eggs were white and varying shades of brown, with speckles. Both were enormous compared with mine, which had a thick shell and a bright, large yellow-orange yolk, which took up nearly three-quarters of the egg. I ate the eggs in hard-boiled form and fried in a little butter. Horizon came in third. Some of the yolks had slightly metallic flavors, with a hint of fish. Knoll Krest was very good, with a richer, cleaner-tasting yolk. But my chicken, I have to report, carried the day. The gradations of egg flavor are very subtle, which means that freshness can easily tilt the balance. And when it comes to freshness, well, the competition was over before it began. Horizon and Knoll Krest yolks turned slightly dry and mealy with cooking, while my yolks stayed fluffy and moist. The whites had not a hint of rubberiness. No contest. And now that production is in full swing, I can count on five or six eggs a week, although there have been factory rejects. One egg was quail size. Another had a strange squiggle on top, like soft ice cream. But on balance, the chicken has been a consistent, high-quality producer.

It says something about New York that no one in the neighborhood seems to think it's odd to have a chicken in the backyard. People have noticed. But they don't pay much attention. After all, it could be a snarling, frothing pit bull. In the scheme of things, a chicken blends in. And it certainly settles one age-old question. It's the chicken that came first. Then came the egg.

William Grimes

But the chicken didn't stay. A few weeks later, William Grimes wrote this article:

I have bad news. The chicken is gone.

The plump black hen that appeared out of nowhere on a cold winter day disappeared just as mysteriously a week ago. Like Garbo retiring from motion pictures, she left at the height of her popularity, well on her way to becoming the most photographed, most talked about chicken of our time. Admittedly, there's not a lot of competition in this particular arena (the San Diego Chicken does not count). But still. She was my little star. And now she's gone.

If only she knew what a stir she caused. Her arrival, and her thoughtful production of fresh eggs, started a new, rural chapter in my life. Then I wrote about her, and things really took off. My mailbag filled to the bursting point with letters offering advice on the proper care and feeding of chickens, along with fascinating chicken facts. (Didn't I know their combs can freeze?) I learned about the role of calcium in egg formation, the importance of fresh drinking water and what to call the color of my eggs. It's not ecru, it's whole wheat. One caller wanted to know if I'd like to adopt a couple of white leghorn roosters.

Never have so many worried so much about one hen. Fans of the chicken, disturbed that she did not have a name, wrote with suggestions. I thought Vivian had a certain sultry appeal. Henrietta seemed cute. But folks, you will have to do better than Henny Penny.

The media jumped in. National Public Radio quizzed me about the chicken for one of its weekend programs. "My producer wants to know, could you go out and hold the telephone up to the chicken so we can hear it?" the interviewer asked at one point. I agree that would have been a great moment in radio. Unfortunately, I don't have a 100-foot cord on my telephone. The Associated Press sent a photographer to capture the chicken's many moods. Actually, she had two moods, but this photographer got both of them.

Book publishers called to sign that hen to a contract. The *New York Post*, ever helpful, assigned a reporter to see if keeping a chicken in the city is legal. (The answer is yes.)

My life was spinning out of control. For John Reed it was the Bolshevik Revolution. For Woodward and Bernstein it was Watergate. For me, it was the chicken, the story that surpassed the sum total of every other story I've ever written. But then it all stopped.

The facts are these. On Wednesday afternoon the chicken was observed resting comfortably in her nest beneath the backyard pine tree. In retrospect, she seemed a little more subdued than usual. But the orange eye that regarded me was bright and lively.

The chicken showed her usual signs of excitement at the sound of dry cat food hitting the bowls on the little patio where I feed several neighborhood cats.

When I looked out my kitchen window on Thursday morning, my heart stopped. No chicken. There was no sign of her in my pine tree or the tree next door. She was not pecking and scratching in any of the nearby yards.

I searched for signs of violence but did not find any. The only trace of the chicken was a single black feather near the back door. She was definitely, profoundly missing.

But why?

I do not have a suspicious turn of mind. But it seemed odd that a chicken that had peacefully dwelled in my backyard for more than two months disappeared only a few days after her picture appeared in this newspaper.

I resist the thought that evil walks among us in Astoria. Spring is in the air. Could she be looking for love?

Was she reacting badly to the burdens of celebrity? I know for a fact that she did not like the telephoto lens that the cameraman from the *Times* brought into the backyard.

When the Associated Press showed up a few days later, the chicken may have formed a silent resolution: As of today, I'm looking for a place where I can lay my eggs in peace.

As the anxious hours crawled by, my wife, Nancy, surveyed the neighborhood yards with a pair of high-powered binoculars.

I called one of the chicken's many new friends, a real estate broker from Wilmington, N.C., named Brian West, who has been providing me with chicken expertise, not to mention a small bag of ground oyster shells to help the chicken get her minimum daily requirement of calcium.

Would the chicken return? There was hope, according to Mr. West. "Sometimes they wander off, but usually they come back in a day or two," he said. My spirits lifted. "If it gets to be four or five days, though, there's not much chance that it will return." My spirits sank.

Nancy and I counted the hours. I wandered the neighborhood, peering into yards. I decided not to post a picture and a reward. I envisioned a line down the block, one reward seeker after another with an identical black chicken tucked under his arm.

Once, I thought I heard the chicken delivering one of her high-volume scoldings. The sound faded. I decided it was a rusty pulley on a clothesline.

At this point, with no sign of the chicken after a week, hope wanes.

Nancy and I have been through all the psychological stages associated with a traumatic event of this kind. Did we do something

wrong? Was it our fault? Self-blame turns to anger. Who would kid-
nap a chicken? Anger gives way to fruitless wondering. Where could
the chicken possibly go? But then again, she came from a place
unknown. Why should it seem surprising that she simply upped and
left one day? If only the chicken had known how much better her
life was about to get. On a recent trip to the Midwest, I had found a
feed store and bought a 50-pound bag of chicken feed for the
princely sum of eight dollars.

I sealed the feed up in about 20 Ziploc bags and distributed them
in two suitcases, hoping against hope that the Drug Enforcement
Agency would not be holding me for a lengthy conversation at the
airport. After deciding that the chicken needed a housing upgrade, I
ordered a plastic nest and perch from a chicken-supply site on the
Internet. Mr. West urged me to get two more chickens.

"It's just as easy to take care of three as it is to take care of one,
and having other chickens around would reduce stress on your hen,"
he said. I'm not sure that Mr. West quite realizes what the layout is
here in New York City, but I was giving serious thought to the matter. But were all these improvements too little, too late?

Nancy was distraught. "It really was a big presence in the backyard," she said glumly. I was depressed, too. Far more so than I could
have imagined. We had grown to love the chicken. We also loved
the eggs. Now, I cherish the memories and the letters. An elderly
gentleman told me about a chicken named Mary that used to walk
into his mother's kitchen in Floral Park, Queens, take a seat in its
favorite chair, and spend all day socializing. At sunset it would go
outside and roost in a tree. Julie North Chelminski of Norwalk,
Conn., sent photographs of her flock of chickens, which line up to
lay eggs in the backyard clay oven.

Miriam Katin of Manhattan recalled the sad tale of a chicken she
saw wandering at the corner of Spring and Greene Streets in SoHo.
A sympathetic bystander threw a piece of bagel at the poor thing,
spooking it so badly that it ran into the street, where it was run over
by a passing cyclist.

Many correspondents assured me that my chicken would happily eat just about anything but the plastic yard furniture. Pasta ranked high, and cantaloupe rinds. Apparently, chickens will peck a rind right down to the webbing. In summer, grass clippings would be her delight. My own research finally settled the question of breed. The chicken was a black Australorp, an Australian breed which is known to be a great egg layer.

I was told that chickens like to hear conversation. I began clucking back at the hen. From time to time I'd make small talk. I confided my worries about the worsening political situation in the Middle East, and my fears about the stock market. She listened intently.

Those happy days have come to an end. We have the new nest, and 50 pounds of chicken feed. The cats carry on as before. But the two humans are bereft. If anyone happens to see a fat black hen, tell her this for me. There's a light in the window, and a warm nest at the base of the pine tree.

WHITE HOUSE SQUIRRELS

WASHINGTON, D.C.—It has been a White House problem for 200 years. Some presidents have confronted it head on. Others have fought in self-defense. Right now the Bush administration is trying to make nice, but with mixed results.

The adversary is the small Eastern gray squirrel, which is a familiar pest throughout the United States. But the gray squirrels at the White House are noticeably fatter, sleeker and bolder than their cousins in the rest of the country. And they are a bigger threat, too. They don't just destroy property. They destroy history.

Last fall, White House squirrels ate their way through the bark of an old buckeye tree on the North Lawn that had been planted back when Theodore Roosevelt lived here. The squirrels stripped so many of the top limbs that the tree died and groundskeepers had to cut it down.

So it is surprising to learn that these very same squirrels are fed official government rations of peanuts on the White House grounds.

The reason for the peanuts is not exactly to get the squirrels to stay—although that's one result. The peanuts are given to lure the squirrels away from the tens of thousands of tulip bulbs planted each fall.

"The squirrels were digging them up and actually having a meal," said Irvin Williams, the chief superintendent of the White House grounds. Mr. Williams, 77, has been a gardener at the mansion since the Truman administration, in 1949, when he first began battling gray squirrels. Six years ago, when the squirrels had become so aggressive that they were eating hundreds of tulip bulbs and ruining the perfect rows of spring plantings, Mr. Williams decided to try enticing them away with peanut feeders placed in White House trees.

"I was hoping they would eat enough peanuts that they wouldn't need to eat the tulip bulbs," Mr. Williams said. "But a couple of them liked both."

The peanut feeding program runs from November, when the bulbs are planted, until spring, when the tulips bloom. And it has definitely cut down considerably on the loss of bulbs. But Mr. Williams has noticed that the feeders were a solution that might have created a new problem: more squirrels.

"The word could go out, yes," he said.

This is not the first time that Washington has had a well-fed squirrel problem. Back in 1980, a survey by the National Park Service found that because tourists had been feeding peanuts to squirrels in other parts of the city, downtown had turned into a squirrel food festival. The problem was especially intense in Lafayette Park, across the street from the White House, where the study found more than 100 squirrels in the 8.2-acre park, several times the norm. There were so many squirrels that the trees couldn't fit them all, and many didn't even have a home.

The White House is directly across the street from Lafayette Park, and different presidents have faced the squirrel problem in different ways. Dwight D. Eisenhower despised them because they destroyed his White House putting green, where he practiced playing golf, so he had them trapped and deported to the Maryland countryside. This made squirrel lovers angry. Jimmy Carter also tried to relocate the squirrels, to a similar outcry.

Ronald Reagan, much to the outrage of serious gardeners, famously took an opposite approach. He went so far as to feed the squirrels acorns that he kept in his desk drawer after collecting them on weekends at Camp David. On warm, sunny days the squirrels would gather outside the Oval Office and wait patiently for presents from the president.

The first President Bush, scrapping the Reagan policy, not only put a stop to such handouts but also sent his dog Millie to chase them. The squirrels, he said proudly, "were history."

The Clinton administration pets continued the chase, as have the Bush II dogs, Barney and Spot. But in another sign of a softening of attitudes, the White House this past holiday season featured a papier-mâché squirrel among the first-family pets on display as part of its "All Creatures Great and Small" decorating theme. The squirrel, the first lady's office said, was a tribute to those that had been "both pets and pests" to White House families for the past two centuries.

Elisabeth Bumiller

FREE WILLY, REALLY

WESTMAN ISLANDS, Iceland—Keiko the whale is a movie star. He is the whale used in the movie *Free Willy* where he played a whale who wanted to return to the wild.

In the movie, he broke out of captivity where he'd been taught to do tricks for humans, and found his "pod" or family out in the sea. In real life, Keiko was given the chance to do the same thing. He was taken to a beautiful secluded sea area in Iceland where his trainers tried to teach him to hunt and communicate like a wild whale. But unlike the movie, Keiko wasn't interested in the wild. It seems his "pod," his family, is made up of humans.

His trainers (who came to Iceland with him, from Oregon) have never seen him catch a live fish for himself. He will do it to please them, but only because he's rewarded with a dead herring or a pat on the nose.

He has played with pods of orcas in the open ocean, but he doesn't stay with them. He makes sounds, but it's not clear they speak the same language. And although his trainers have tried to teach him how to hunt like a wild orca—diving fathoms under a pack of herring, herding them into a ball, then stunning them with tail slaps and roaring through them, eating all the way—he just doesn't get it. In fact the only real exercise he gets is being run through his old movie tricks.

He lives in an area of the sea that has an 800-foot underwater net around it, because his trainers thought he would have to be penned in at first to keep him from running wild. But that was years ago, when he first arrived. Storms have torn holes in his net since then, big enough to drive a truck (or an orca) through, and yet he has stayed inside, near his steel fish pails and his human friends.

Some who study orcas say that the net should be pulled down completely, and his trainers should stop giving him fish, so he will have to fend for himself. But others say he would probably just become a nuisance, begging for handouts from the fishing fleet in the nearby town harbor. He has already frightened the wits out of a bird hunter in a small boat, and once followed a cruise ship when he was supposed to be searching for his family.

It's not that he hasn't tried. He just seems to have trouble making friends. One summer he swam close by different pods for up to three days and played a sort of tag with some of the younger whales. Sometimes the pods were interested in him, sometimes they weren't, but he always ended up swimming away. One day, in the middle of playing, he bellowed suddenly and loudly, scaring off 18 other whales. None of his trainers could figure out why.

And it's not like his trainers haven't tried. To encourage him to hunt, they once stopped feeding him completely (normally they give him about 100 pounds of fish a day)! But after a week they worried he would starve so they started to feed him again.

"He's a great whale," said Jim Horton, one of his handlers with long Sea World experience. "Not a mean bone in his body. Really intelligent, really likes to work with you. Some whales get aggressive, bite your flippers—not him. Great personality."

Donald G. McNeil, Jr.

MONKEYS EVERYWHERE

NIKKO, Japan—At a mountain highway rest stop, tourists were browsing in a souvenir shop and lining up to ride a red-topped gondola to a snowy peak.

Suddenly, word spread through the parking lot: a robbery.

An intruder had jumped through the open door of a car and was rummaging through the interior.

Finally, the car owner offered the thief exactly what he wanted: a ripe banana. With razor-sharp teeth slicing through both the peel and the fruit, the Japanese monkey bounded off.

"There is one monkey that will sit in the road, betting that the car will stop, then he will jump on the hood and demand food," said Tomoaki Matsuo, a freelance television reporter who makes his living filming monkey encounters in this resort town 75 miles north of Tokyo. Others try to jump through open windows of cars moving at close to 20 miles an hour. "The cars almost get into accidents," he said.

Monkeys are spreading across Japan. There weren't many here after World War II—only about 15,000. But the number has increased tenfold in half a century, reaching 150,000 today. In contrast, Japan's human population is expected to drop by half this century, to 65 million.

"If people just let the monkeys reproduce themselves, Japan would be the archipelago of the monkeys in 2200," said Kunio Watanabe, a professor of primate sociology at Kyoto University. "But I don't think that Japanese are that patient."

In fact the Japanese are getting frustrated. Two years ago, Nikko became the first town in Japan to ban the feeding of monkeys. Some mothers now drive their children to school for fear of monkey attacks. "It just gets worse and worse," complained Toki Kaneda, a resident of the Chuzenji Lake section who closed her souvenir store because of monkey theft. "We haven't been able to leave the windows of our second-floor rooms open for years."

There are also more violent ways of fighting back. Nationwide, the number of monkeys killed by humans has soared over the last 25 years to about 10,000 a year today.

Nevertheless, like coyotes in the United States, monkey numbers in Japan keep increasing. With monkey bands moving from mountain areas to farm areas to villages their diet has changed making them larger and more aggressive. They root through trash cans, says Teruo Kanaya, a hotel worker, "they have gotten bigger from eating Western food, like McDonald's, greasy, fatty food."

One of the reasons they like the farm areas is because many of the farmers are gone. There are far fewer farmers in Japan then there were years ago, and now the land is empty and there are no farmers (or farm dogs) to chase the monkeys away. Farmers who stay behind often wonder if they are growing vegetables only to provide monkeys with buffet salad bars. A new book, *Protecting Mountain Fields from Monkeys*, contains the latest in antimonkey technology, including electric fences and 12-foot-high nets.

The police are developing new ways to keep the monkeys away, too. In some rural villages there are rewards of up to $1,000 for the capture of a particularly destructive monkey troop. And in cities, where there are news reports about monkeys causing trouble, police officers have formed monkey posses, patrolling streets with nets and bananas tied to poles.

James Brooke

Possum Festival

ARCADIA, La.—You can still visit the highway site just south of town where six law officers riddled Bonnie and Clyde with bullets 58 years ago. You can sample Snuffy's Pizza, billed as "The best cotton-pickin' pizza y'all ever ett."

But unless Rodney Cook comes to his senses or local businessmen succeed in keeping his dream alive, you may not be able to attend the annual Possum Festival in Arcadia ever again.

Thereby hangs a tale common to thousands of towns throughout the South, where an annual salute to some beloved food, creature or little known hero tends to take on a life of its own.

Like the Clute Mosquito Festival in Texas, Hillbilly Days in Pikeville, Ky., Swine Time in Climax, Ga., and other small-town festivals throughout the South, the Possum Festival started small, 10 years ago, when Mr. Cook started wondering why all those dead possums end up squashed down the middle of the highway.

"I got to looking at all the furballs in the road," said Mr. Cook, referring to the familiar roadside aftermath of one-car, one-possum collisions. Other endangered animals have charities, he reckoned. Save the Whales. Help the Egrets. And from the looks of them, possums were certainly in danger. "You can collect all this money for ducks and send it off, and they just fly over you in the fall going South," Mr. Cook said. So I just decided we needed to help possums, so I formed Possums Unlimited, or P.U. for short."

Things began slowly with a handful of members, $2.89 lifetime memberships in P.U. and a gala inaugural banquet in downtown Arcadia. Mr. Cook said he sold only 10 tickets but 200 or 300 people showed up.

Since then, the Possum Festival has become a major annual event attracting up to 4,000 people, with events like a "preach-off," where various clergymen, ordained or self-appointed, hold a possum funeral.

There are T-shirts—Batpossum, Ninja Possum, "Run over to the Possum Festival"—and annual posters, this year featuring a possum in a '57 Chevrolet tooling down the road leaving squashed people lying behind. Charities get the proceeds, about $120,000 in nine years, Mr. Cook said. And unlike many festivals, he said, this one makes a point of not snacking on the honoree.

"See, we're in the protection business," he said. "We've got a possum cookbook, but the only thing we condone eating is roadkill. The tax assessor here, he used to get two possums and fatten them up for Thanksgiving every year, and we broke him of the habit, converted him. He's a changed man. He's turned to turkey."

Mr. Cook says he's interested in promoting some of the little-known ways possums can be beneficial. "We advertise compass possums," he said. "You can carry them hunting, and if you get lost, just turn it loose, and he'll head for the nearest road."

But, as Mr. Cook has learned, putting on an annual festival is no small job. He said he had lost money doing this, and after nine years, he's ready to stop. "You do get burned out," he said. "A festival, it takes probably three, four, five months to get ready for one. And I live possum the year around. I mean, it's Possum Day every day for me."

Mr. Cook says that although he's serious about getting out of the festival business, he plans to continue with Possums Unlimited. Even that involvement may have peaked, however, now that he's found the answer to the ultimate question in possumdom: why so many commit highway hari-kari.

"We've found out the reason they're in the highway is incoming car tires sound like a crate of apples overturning," he said. "They do like fruit."

Peter Applebome

LLAMA FARMER

CORVALLIS, Mont.—In the economic history of American llamas, there was a time when these big-eared, furry cousins of the camel were not in need of Charlene Hakes's help.

But that was several years ago, when everyone who was anyone (or, at least, anyone who was an animal rancher) wanted one, when a good llama could sell for $5,000 and a male with the right genes could command 10 times that price.

No more. The market for llamas, as packing animals and sources of fur, has crashed, and some animals are being sold off for cheap meat or even abandoned in pockets of the West where they were raised. So Ms. Hakes has stepped in, railing against what she calls the "throwaway llama" culture and beginning a personal crusade to save them by taking in llamas that have been given up by their owners.

There is certainly a place for the sure-footed llamas, explained Ms. Hakes, 47, who was a rancher and a dog groomer before she was a llama rescuer, and who still does both those other things. They make terrific pack animals, carrying huge, heavy loads of camping equipment on their backs, so trekking companies from Alaska to the Adirondacks use them on guided trips. Their fur is strong, warm and richly colored, eminently usable for sweaters and blankets. They make excellent sheep guards. A few golf courses even use them as caddies because they are good at carrying clubs.

Llamas can also be good pets, but only if properly trained. Often when the telephone rings at her house, Ms. Hakes said, "Someone calls up and says, 'I have this llama, and it's not what I thought it was going to be.'

"I tell people that if what you want is a fuzzy, cuddly animal to lick your face, then get a dog. In fact, treating a baby llama like a puppy is what creates the problem. If you kiss them and hug them and blow on their faces, then once they get older, they're just in your face all day. They won't leave you alone. They'll push you. They'll butt you. They'll hurt you. They become unmanageable."

So Ms. Hakes, who has 46 llamas in the backyard of her five-acre ranch and has cared for about 300 in all since taking up her mission, asks some very specific questions when people inquire not about getting rid of a problem llama but about buying one from her.

"I say, 'O.K., let's talk llama,'" she said. "'What do you want to do with this llama? What do you expect of this llama? Do you have housing for this llama?'"

She will also send a prospective buyer a video about how to care for it, and explain that llamas are herd animals that can become very anxious if no other animals are around.

Their reputation for spitting is well deserved, she said, although they generally spit only at one another. Sometimes they do so just because they are annoyed, but other times it is part of an elaborate ritual aimed at establishing who is top llama, a ritual that also includes butting chests and pointing ears.

Anyone who looks after llamas will occasionally get caught in the spitting crossfire, conceded Ms. Hakes, an energetic woman with sandy hair and oval wire-rimmed glasses.

"It doesn't hurt," she said. "It does stink, depending on what they've been eating."

But most of the time llamas are peaceful and playful, and they make little noise, generally just a humming sound. Ms. Hakes's llamas arrive from all over the Bitterroot region of Montana. Their names include Sky, Myia, Locca, Luxor, Blue Moon, Twizzy, Emma, Toby and Redford (as in Robert). They are frequently joined by Ms. Hakes's dog, a black Lab named Nokia. (As in the cell phone company: "I just like the sound of the name," she said.)

It is possible that her company, Silhouette Llamas, could be a moneymaker one day, if the market rebounds and ranchers want to breed llama again. In the meantime, caring for them gives her the feeling of having done a bit of good on this earth.

"I love these guys," she explained, gesturing out across the ranch. "I know I can't save the world. But I can save some llamas."

Sam Howe Verhovek

ICELAND ALLIGATORS

HUSAVIK, Iceland—Here on Iceland's northern shore, everything is icy. The arctic grouse are already wearing their white winter coats. Snow is everywhere. Woo-hoo! say the city fathers. What an excellent place to raise alligators.

Alligators? Are they serious? Actually, the idea of turning Husavik into the Everglades of the Arctic is not as wild as it sounds. They call it the "Krokodil Plan," and it is a creative idea that might help this small town survive.

Husavik is a town of only 2,500 people, which is very big by Iceland's standards. Still, other rural fishing towns this size are dying as the number of fish shrink in the oceans and young adults move away to the city of Reykjavik, the capital.

Husavik is striving mightily to avoid that fate. Among its survival plans: retrofitting three old oak fishing boats and attracting 24,000 tourists who travel here to watch the whales; opening a new whaling museum (it started in a tiny former fish freezer but soon moved to a not so tiny former sheep slaughterhouse); going into a brand-new industry—cutting wood for floors—because it costs next to nothing to steam dry lumber here.

The reason steam drying is free is the same reason the alligators might like it in Husavik: the steam comes from Iceland's volcanoes. The town gets all of its heating for houses and most of its electricity out of the ground. About 12 miles inland, there is a geothermal field whose deepest wells produce water at 248 degrees Fahrenheit.

This superheated water flows through an insulated high-pressure pipeline to a turbine plant that generates nearly all of the town's electricity. Then it runs through a network of house radiators and frost-fighting pipes beneath the sidewalks. (Wouldn't you like a set of those pipes when it's time to shovel your own front walk?)

Hot water is not the only thing nature supplies to the plant. There is cold water running through it, too, from melted glaciers, and that water is used as a coolant. By the time it makes its way through the entire plant it has warmed up to between 77 to 86 degrees. It is then piped out of the plant into a couple of man-made ponds. Husavikians swim there in winter, enjoying the nice warm water.

The mayor of Husavik thinks these swimmers belong in the local (indoor) swimming pool, and that the ponds should be filled with alligators. The gators could live on waste from the local fish-packing plants, among other things. And the tourists who come to see the whales would really LOVE the alligators. There's no reason to worry that the alligators would crawl out of their ponds and terrorize people, because it would be too cold for them to move.

There is only one problem. The experts from Florida who have been giving advice to the Icelanders warn that baby alligators might eat fish scraps but grown-up alligators will demand more. The mayor has a solution to that one, too. Once the gators stop eating the fish scraps, he says, the people will start eating the gators.

Bringing in animals from other places is tradition in Iceland, he explains. The arctic fox is one of the only animals that is native to the country. Reindeer were imported from elsewhere long, long ago, as were the popular chestnut horses with blond hair and the sheep that look like cotton balls with horns.

Donald G. McNeil, Jr.

A DOG'S LIFE

ASTORIA, Queens—Survival is his full-time occupation. He is homeless and moves stiffly, like a rusty garden gate.

Mondays are the worst. That is when the pickings are slimmest. The trash man comes Tuesday and Friday to Crescent Street in Astoria, Queens, and Wednesday and Saturday to 26th Street, the next block over. That leaves three skinny days without garbage. Three skinny days of eating on the kindness of strangers.

Sundays are good. People in the neighborhood bring him paper plates loaded with leftovers or else they toss bits of bread and ham from their windows. There is a hole in a fence that he can wiggle through and if he is especially hungry he will find the scraps on the ground. But on Mondays, people are concerned with jobs and schoolbooks and they pay him little mind. Mondays are the worst.

He appears to be middle-aged and of mixed lineage. Part German shepherd, part something else. He is smallish, but his ears are large and batlike; his quarters are round and muscular. He walks with a hanged head and steps off the path when people come around.

He is a stray dog, nothing more. The people of the neighborhood feel sorry for him, knowing he has gone from comfortable circumstances to bad ones. He is harmless enough and for these reasons they have not contacted the authorities. "He don't ask for money and he don't bother no one," said Bill Nestor, a retired fender and body man. "People smile when they see him."

The teenagers call him Trixie—as in the tricky way he appears and disappears. The superstitious call him Diablo (which means "the devil" in Spanish) for the same reason. Some call him Lucky. Lydia Rivera calls him Abraham. "I don't know what his real name is," she said the other day, smiling as he skulked by. "But Abraham, that's a name from the Bible. It just came to me. Abraham. He seems to answer to it. He's a sweet little man. I leave food over there by the bushes where he sleeps."

He has grown visibly older since he started sleeping under the bushes three years ago. His hair is patchy in some places. He walks with a jerky, crooked gait. He was hit by a car last summer. He does not look shabby the way that most tramps do.

Abraham's origins are murky. The neighborhood people know that he once belonged to an old man who lived in one of the apartments on Crescent Street. They used to see the old man and Abraham taking evening walks along 20th Avenue, on the sidewalk that separates the apartments from the power plant. The old man may have died because the old man is not around anymore and Abraham lives under the bush.

No one seems to remember the old man's name. "That's New York," said Eugene Perez, a handyman who works at a nearby apartment complex and knows Abraham as well as anyone. "Who knows their neighbors' names? Everybody knows the dog, though, because you're not allowed to have pets of your own here. He sort of belongs to everybody and sort of belongs to himself."

The dogcatcher has been prowling around the last few weeks. He's given Abraham a good contest, Mr. Perez said. But the dog is just too clever. The handymen leave the hinged doors to the crawl spaces open for Abraham, and when he sees the dogcatcher coming, the dog hides under the building. "What are they going to do when they get him?" Mr. Perez asked. "Take him to the pound and put him to sleep. They should leave him alone. People here love him and he's having a good life."

Charlie LeDuff

After Charlie LeDuff's story ran, people all over the country read about Abraham. So many people wrote and called, that Charlie LeDuff wrote a second story a few days later:

They called from Los Angeles and Miami. They called from Wood-stock, N.Y., and Stamford, Conn. After reading about Abraham they all wanted to help.

There were lifetime offers of food. A woman volunteered to pay his veterinary bills. One man of means considered sending his driver and limousine in pursuit of the furry tramp. They were concerned, but their interest ended with that phone call.

Until Thursday, when John Contino, a retired telephone repair-man who spends his days rescuing stray and abused dogs, took it upon himself to track down Abraham in his five-block territory in Astoria. Mr. Contino runs a one-man one-dog rescue squad called Mighty Mutts out of his house in Brooklyn. He will take in any dog that needs help, help it get used to living around people, then place it in a loving home.

It was a Thursday afternoon as the snow began to fall when Mr. Contino called *The New York Times* by cellular phone. "I've been following him for four hours," Mr. Contino said, "but I got him." He was euphoric. "He's one of the smartest dogs I've come across, but I got him."

He cornered Abraham with the help of Clint, his red-nosed pit bull, and then lassoed him with a rod and rope. In the background during the call, shouts and sobs could be heard from a group of neighbors who had fed and protected the dog since his master disappeared three years ago.

"I'm having trouble convincing them that I'm not taking him to the pound," Mr. Contino said.

Since running wild, he has had many different names, none of which he chose. The neighbors called him Abraham, Trixie, Lucky, Poncho. And when the dogcatcher called him, he just ran. A very clever dog. Now he is named Tommy, rechristened by Mr. Contino in gratitude to a man who helped to trap him. With the neighbors in tow, Tommy was taken to the veterinarian for a checkup.

Tommy has worms and a growth on his right flank, but his teeth are quite good for a dog who has lived outside so long, said Dr. Salvatore J. Pernice of the Brooklyn Veterinary Group in Bensonhurst.

"It's going to take a while to get him used to people," Mr. Contino said. Maybe three months. Maybe a year. "He was tortured living out there on the streets."

SCHOOL

Dai Manju Goes to School

YEJUAO, China—Dai Manju is a sixth-grade girl whose eyes shine when she talks about how she loves school. But, at the age of 13, she has already had to drop out of elementary school four times.

It is not that she minds the unheated dormitory crammed with bunks, where she and other girls sleep two or three to a bed on the six nights a week they are at school. Nor did she drop out because of annoyance at having to help with the vegetable garden that the pupils and teachers keep to feed themselves.

"My parents were ill, and they said they couldn't afford sending me to school," said Dai Manju as she stood in front of the crudely built classroom where she is a star pupil. "Since I am the oldest child, my parents asked me to drop out and help with the housework."

Tuition at the school is only $13 a year, including a spot in a shared bed and three meals a day. But in this remote and backward part of Central China, where the peasants barely earn $60 a year,

$13 is more than most people can afford. Dai Manju's family of five is one of the poorer ones and they own almost nothing—not a radio, not even a bicycle or a watch.

Her tiny school here in Yejuao (pronounced YEH joo OW) is like nothing American children have ever seen. Classrooms are unheated, so that in winter the children's fingers get so cold it is hard to hold a pencil. The dormitory rooms have no running water, and instead of bathrooms they have outhouses. The toilets consist of three holes in the ground, surrounded by a low wall; they smell terrible and, because there are no lights, they are dark at night. There is no place to take a bath or a shower, and in winter the students wear the same clothes all week.

It would surprise many American students to learn that even with all these problems, school spirit at the Yejuao Elementary School is better than at many American schools. There is almost no vandalism in Dai Manju's school, and teachers are honored and respected. When teachers walk into the room the students stand at attention and welcome them. The most popular students are not the athletes or the trouble-makers but the ones who work the hardest.

Poor as these schools are, the children who attend think they are the lucky ones. In all of China, more than half of children never graduate from junior high school and an alarming number of rural children do not learn how to read and write.

"A week after the beginning of school in the spring term this year, we found that 50 of our 170 pupils had dropped out," the principal said. That was when he and the teachers moved into high gear, proving that while rural Chinese schools may lack tape recorders, gymnasiums and toilet paper, they have endless energy and commitment to their students.

The entire school staff went door to door, begging parents to keep the children in school. If one trip did not work, they went again and again, sometimes trudging two or three hours over mountain trails to the children's homes. Chinese teachers often have to do this—and more—to help keep children in school. At another elementary school in a nearby village, one boy was a bed-wetter and dropped out of school after the other boys refused to allow him to share their beds and there was not enough room for him to have a bed all his own. So the principal there persuaded the child to come back and offered to share his own bed with the child. The boy promptly wet the principal's bed and quilt. Afterward, the principal woke the boy at 2 A.M. every day and took him to the outhouse. The boy stopped wetting his bed and was able to return to the dormitory.

At Dai Manju's school, the home visits from the teachers worked, and soon 46 of the 50 pupils were back in school. Among them was Dai Manju herself, whose parents agreed to let her return only because her teachers, knowing how poor her parents are, offered to pay the little girl's $13 tuition themselves. Her dreams are still alive.

"I want to go on to junior high school next year," she said, explaining her hope of becoming a crafts teacher when she grows up. Junior high will be more expensive, though—the fee is $4 more a year—and she worries if her parents will allow her to attend.

Nicholas D. Kristof

Four months later, the reporter, Nicholas Kristof, went back to visit Dai Manju and her school. This is what he found:

YEJUAO, China—This year, at the age of 14, Dai Manju will become the first person in her family ever to graduate from elementary school. It will be such a big event for her family that they might even celebrate by eating a bit of meat—something they are too poor to do very often.

"Oh, we can't eat meat regularly," said the girl's father, Dai Han-ren, who said foods like pork and chicken were too expensive to eat once a week or even once a month. "Our custom is to eat meat only on special festivals."

School was too expensive for his daughter, too, he said, until the teachers agreed to help. Then more help came from a most unexpected place. Readers of *The New York Times* read Dai Manju's story and sent her money. One reader, because of a mix-up at the bank, sent much more than she had planned. The woman wrote a check for $100, but before the bank could send that check to China it had to be converted from American dollars into Chinese yuan. That's when the bank made a simple math mistake—they forgot the decimal point—and sent $10,000 worth of yuan instead of $100 worth.

Ten thousand dollars is more than peasants like the Dai's could earn in 100 years. So the money was used to provide scholarships to nearly half of the students (the amounts ranged from 50 cents to a few dollars) and to build a new school in the next village where the old school was falling apart.

Because even $10,000 was not enough for the whole new school, much of the actual building was done by hundreds of local parents. "One of my kids is at the Yellow Mud Elementary School, and so I wanted to pitch in to build the new school," said Zhou Qishui, a barefoot 48-year-old peasant who was working with several dozen other parents on the site of the new building. He contributed $2 to the project and is also donating 20 days of his labor.

More than 10 years passed and Nicholas Kristof went back once again. Dai Manju was now an adult, and her family was still living in the village where she grew up. Many things about their life there had changed:

GAOSHAN, China—When I first met the Dais in 1990 Gaoshan had no electricity and was a two-hour hike from the nearest dirt road. The Dais shared their mud-brick house with their pig, and they owned nothing: no watch, no bicycle, no change of clothes.

When I decided to seek out the Dai family again I thought I would find them still living amid desperate poverty. But then I came to the end of the old dirt road—and found that the path had been extended a few years ago so that now it is possible to drive all the way to Gaoshan. Every home in the village now has electricity. Two families even have telephones.

As for the Dais, they are living in a new six-room house, made of concrete. The pig lives outside. The parents proudly showed me their stove, television and electric fan.

Dai Manju turned out to have graduated from high school and then from technical school in accounting, and such lofty academic credentials are no longer uncommon in Gaoshan. She and her two siblings are working in Guangdong Province, all earning $125 a month or more—what her father earned in a year.

IT LOOKS LIKE THE LUNCH MENU. IT'S REALLY YOUR CHILD'S REPORT CARD

Newspaper reporters move to the foreign countries that they cover. Sometimes that can mean new and unusual experiences for the entire family. This is the story written by a correspondent who moved to Italy and enrolled her daughter in the local kindergarten there.

ROME, Italy—The first parents' meeting of the year at my child's Italian public school started off with a warning. We all hunched anxiously over tiny first-grade desks as the teacher rose from her chair and stated solemnly, "I have bad news."

Teachers' strike, typhoid and no textbooks were some of the potential crises that rushed through my head. But what the teacher was worried about drew a gasp of horror from the other parents.

"Your children are not eating," she said sternly. "Some of them don't even touch their second course."

Everybody knows Italians are obsessed with food. My mother is Italian, I spent many childhood summers in Rome and Tuscany, so I was well acquainted, I thought, with the importance of cooking pasta al dente, the moral imperative to throw out day-old mozzarella and never to go swimming less than two hours after lunch.

But even I was unprepared for how a food-centric nation handles education. When my daughter started kindergarten last year, I was surprised to find a huge chart posted on the door, marked with what appeared to be grades. On closer inspection, the chart turned out to be a scorecard of the day's lunch achievements.

Every day, next to each child's name, the teacher marked down what she ate, and how well.

EMMA: Primo (first course): Pasta con pomodoro (pasta with tomato sauce). Tutto. Ottimo. (Ate all. Excellent.)

Secondo (second course): Scaloppine di vitello (veal scallops). Meta. Molto bene. (Half. Very good.)

Contorno (side dish): Patate bollite e fagiolini (boiled potato and beans). Poco. Bene. (A little. Good.)

Dolce (dessert): Pera cotta (stewed pear). Niente. Maggiore impegno. (None. Needs work.)

Fraud and corruption scams are a constant theme in Italian newspapers. Almost every day, somewhere in Italy there is a scandal over rigged lotteries, sports "doping" or government corruption. But the one kind of scandal guaranteed to make the front pages has the word "mensa" in it. Mensa, in Italian, means school cafeteria, and any story that suggests that children are being cheated of their culinary due unleashes mass hysteria.

Last month, 13 people, many of them high-ranking city administrators, were arrested in Milan after a local catering company was found to be providing substandard food to city-run hospitals and schools. After the Milan story broke, parents gathered in angry groups outside our school, here in Rome, militantly ready to storm the school kitchen.

"My son brought home an apple that I swear was bruised," one mother said urgently. "How do we know they are not buying second-rate produce and pocketing the profits?"

The school held an emergency meeting to address those concerns. I have yet to talk to another mother about reading skills or after-school programs. We do occasionally gather over espresso at the cafe next to the school to debate the school cook's ability to produce a satisfying "suppli di riso."

So far, I have been lucky enough never to get an urgent summons from the school about a broken bone or high fever. But once, early on, I was on assignment in Venice when my husband got a panicked call from Emma's kindergarten teacher, asking him to come over right away. His Italian wasn't very fluent, so as he raced over, he called me on my cell phone to urge me to catch an earlier flight home. I did. The emergency was, of course, food-related. Emma, who at the time still didn't speak Italian, wept when the cafeteria lady sprinkled parmigiano on her pasta and she refused to eat it.

It should go without saying that the school day begins with "merenda," the Italian word for snack, except that it is not considered optional. Mothers are expected to provide their children every morning with a fresh slice of pizza bianca to tide them over until lunch.

In the afternoon, the kindergarten teacher distributes apples and slices of bread and nutella, a chocolate and hazelnut spread. (Child obesity rates in Italy are increasing, but they are lower than in the United States, 22.5 percent vs. 25 to 27 percent.)

After 18 months, I have gotten used to all this. When I get home from work, I never ask my child what she did in school. Like every other Italian parent, I remove the soiled cloth napkin from her book bag and ask, "What did you eat for lunch today?"

Alessandra Stanley

Reading at 8 Months? That Was Just the Start

STONY BROOK, N.Y.—Last month, Alia Sabur, a college senior, arrived at her final exam for Applied Math 301 at 7 P.M. The room was nearly empty. "What were you thinking?" asked her professor, Alan Tucker. The test was actually scheduled from 5 to 7:30 P.M.

Alia was thinking, "Time to get started." She sat down and finished in 15 minutes. Afterwards, her mother, Julie, recalls, "She looked very happy. I said, 'Alia, 15 minutes? Did you check it?' Alia said, 'It's fine, Mom.'" And it was. Another perfect score for Alia Sabur. As her professor wrote in an e-mail message, "Maybe you should show up late for all your finals."

Alia is just 13, the age when most students are in the seventh grade. But Alia will earn her undergraduate degree from the State University at Stony Brook this spring. She has been stunning people for a long time, beginning with her parents, who thought it odd when she started reading words at 8 months old.

Professor Harold Metcalf taught her in physics her freshman year, when she was 10 years old. "I was skeptical," he says. "Such a little girl. Then the second or third class, she asked a question. I realized, this girl understands. I've occasionally seen this at 15 or 16, but not 10."

And not just math and physics. She is an accomplished clarinetist. Ricardo Morales, principal clarinet for the Metropolitan Opera orchestra, is her teacher. He recalls two years ago, preparing her to play the Mozart Concerto for Clarinet.

"Such a monumental piece," he says. "It requires a beautiful sound, beautiful phrasing, a solid technical foundation. You must sing through the instrument. She does! It was child's play for her." Literally.

The Rockland Symphony billed her as "Alia Sabur, child prodigy, age 11."

Her professors say that beyond an extraordinary mind, what makes Alia special is a hunger to learn, a willingness to work hard and an emotional balance well beyond her years. This would seem to be every parent's dream, but for a long time it was not. How do you find the proper school setting for a child who read *Charlotte's Web* at age 2? ("I didn't read it by reading," Alia said. "I looked at it and absorbed it.")

When Alia was in kindergarten, her mother quit as a reporter for a local cable TV station to manage her only child's education. By 5, Alia had finished the elementary reading curriculum at her Long Island public school. By second grade, she traveled to middle school for eighth-grade math. ("The kids were so big," she recalled.)

Things fell apart in the fourth grade. Public school officials said they could no longer accommodate Alia's special needs, Ms. Sabur said, and even Manhattan's best private schools felt she was too advanced. Colleges they consulted would not accept so young a child.

"I spent fourth grade sitting by myself reading," Alia recalled. "The teacher would say, 'Find something to do. I'm teaching the class.'" (The year wasn't a total waste; Alia did earn her black belt in karate.)

Finally, Ms. Sabur got help at Stony Brook. "Their attitude was 'We're a public university, it's our duty to find a way,'" she said. Alia's mother accompanied the 10-year-old to college every day. Alia took her stuffed animals to Physics 251. She never took notes in lectures—"The concepts are the important part," she said.

Though she can read a novel at 100 pages an hour—"70 to 80 if it's Dickens"—Alia did not take freshman English until junior year.

"We wanted to wait until she was at least 12 to talk about the Holocaust, drugs, misery," Ms. Sabur said. "The goal wasn't to graduate quickly. We wanted a balanced education to challenge Alia." Recently, Alia won an honor society award as top academic senior.

Ms. Sabur knows what people think when they hear of her daughter. "They think, 'social misfit,'" she said. Ms. Sabur has worked to help Alia find friends her own age. Twice a week, she schedules an art class and lunch with a group of ninth-grade girls. And while Alia said it felt a little forced at first—"I didn't know a lot of the middle school stuff they were talking about"—she now counts three of the girls as friends.

On campus, Alia is closest with foreign students, Constantinos Constantinou, 23, from Cypress, and Taiga Inoue, 21, of Japan. "People like Alia and me, we don't fit in with the main group," Mr. Constantinou said. "We have to mix with others who don't fit in." They share a language, physics. "All I have to do," he said, "is write one equation. How did this guy come to it? It's so beautiful, so perfect."

Charles Fortmann, Alia's research adviser, treats her like a colleague. She is helping him with a project on protein folding that could someday lead to a medical breakthrough. As Alia explained, if they can understand precisely how a protein works, they might be able to understand why in some cases—like Alzheimer's—it malfunctions.

"Here we have A squared," Dr. Fortmann said in a recent session. "I'd like you to do a unit conversion—can we get back to something that makes sense like eV?" Dr. Fortmann drew several diagrams on the board, but Alia did not take a note, just nodded. He describes Alia as "a quiet person but you have to listen carefully. If she mentions a problem with something I'm doing, there probably is."

Dr. Fortmann hopes Alia will continue her graduate work at

Stony Brook, but says, "she could go any place—Stanford, M.I.T., Princeton."

That will partly depend on money, said Ms. Sabur, who drives an '86 Honda with 186,000 miles. She and her husband, Mark, a retired engineer, have found that creating an education for Alia is expensive.

Alia is thinking of doing doctoral research next year, attending a music conservatory and performing.

"You know how Einstein said the speed of light is constant," she said. "People are starting to think nowadays—and I'm one of them—that it's not. That's something I'd like to look at."

Michael Winerip

ONE ANGRY BOY

ORANGETOWN, N.Y.—The incident at Cottage Lane School began with the quiet, private anger of a 10-year-old boy. His teacher had kept the class inside at recess to punish students for talking, and he was mad.

The boy, Misha Spivack, opened his "Personal Response Journal," where students record their thoughts, and described his fifth-grade teacher with an expletive for buttocks. After the teacher, Lawanda Lane, read it, she told school officials, who arranged with Misha's parents for him to take the next day off and then switch teachers.

With Misha out of the classroom, Ms. Lane spent time discussing the incident with the other students. School officials say she started that conversation to calm the class; Misha's parents say she did it to get dirt on Misha. Whatever the reason, the conversation started rumors, and word spread that Misha had pipe-bomb recipes from the

Internet and had talked of bringing a gun to school. Worried parents called the teacher.

Suddenly, a frenzy was under way, turning educators into investigators and parents into defense lawyers. Ms. Lane alerted the police. A detective visited the Spivacks and found that whatever Misha might have claimed, the family had neither a gun nor a computer, much less Internet access. When Misha got to school that morning, he was the talk of Cottage Lane. Then a student spotted the knife.

It was a souvenir from a camping trip that Misha said he had worn for some time on a key chain attached to his belt. It has a nail file, little scissors and a one-and-a-half-inch blade. The student told a teacher. Misha was suspended pending a hearing.

"We don't tolerate knives in school," said Eileen K. Gress, superintendent of the South Orangetown Central School District.

Worry swept the community. The principal, superintendent and school board members all got calls. At the high school, students asked Anton Spivack, 14, whether his little brother had stabbed someone.

When the disciplinary hearing was held, a student testified that Misha told him he "didn't like" their teacher "and he wanted to hurt her." The boy also quoted Misha as saying "he might bring a gun to school." In an interview with a newspaper reporter Misha didn't deny talking tough. "I probably did say that," he said. "But I don't think I was so specific. I wouldn't say pipe bomb because I don't even know what a pipe bomb is." He contends many classmates say things like: "God, I think this school sucks. I wish we could blow it up."

Misha was suspended for a total of eight days. The superintendent sent a letter to all the parents in the school saying that despite the pocket knife and tough talk, Misha never "intended any harm to the students, staff or school."

His suspension over, Misha finds himself treated like a dangerous outsider at his school. He rides to and from school alone in a van, not on a school bus. An aide has been with him much of the time. And for a while, he said, he was not allowed in regular student bathrooms.

Misha's mother said she does not approve of her son's language, but she defended his right to an opinion, particularly in a journal he expected would be private. She and her husband moved their family here for the clean air, open space and good schools. But, she says, the commute was getting to them, and Misha's experience was the last straw. They're moving back to New York City.

Matthew Purdy

A Bumpy Road to a Harvard Degree

***

CAMBRIDGE, Mass.—The title of Brooke Ellison's senior honors thesis—the detailed final paper she wrote to graduate from Harvard University—is "The Element of Hope in Resilient Adolescents." It is about how young people can bounce back from terrible events in their lives, and it contained a lot of scientific data. But she could also have simply titled it: "My Life."

On the first day of seventh grade, Ms. Ellison was struck by a car and doctors told her parents there was little chance she would survive. She did survive, but when she awoke from a coma after 36 hours she found she was a quadriplegic, meaning she could not feel or move anything below her neck. In spite of this, among her first questions were these: "When can I get back to school?" and "Will I be left back?"

She certainly did go back to school and she was definitely not left back. After high school came college—and not just any college, she went to the prestigious Harvard University where she graduated with an A- average and a degree in psychology and biology.

Perhaps the most extraordinary thing about this smiling 21-year-old woman is that she doesn't think that what she does is at all extraordinary, whether it is piloting her wheelchair (as well as the cursor on her computer screen) by touching her tongue to a keypad in a retainer on the roof of her mouth, or being selected by her peers to address them on senior class day before graduation.

"This is just the way my life is," Ms. Ellison said over the clicking of a ventilator that forces air through her trachea and into her lungs 13 times a minute. "I've always felt that whatever circumstances I confront, it's just a question of continuing to live and not letting what I can't do define what I can."

Those looking for a hero in this story, Ms. Ellison suggested, should focus on her mother, Jean Marie, 48, who has sat at her daughter's side in every class since the eighth grade.

After Ms. Ellison was admitted to Harvard, the family decided, reluctantly, that Mrs. Ellison would temporarily leave her husband and teenage son in Stony Brook, N.Y., and move into a dormitory suite with her daughter. The two have hardly been out of earshot, for even a moment, since.

"If I'm with friends or want to be alone," Ms. Ellison said, "she knows when to give me my space."

Mrs. Ellison, whose first—and last—day as a special education teacher was the day of her daughter's accident, has been much more than a 24-hour nurse. Though Ms. Ellison dictated her term papers into a voice-activated computer and did whatever research she could on the Internet, her mother turned the pages of books like *Heart of Darkness* ("I don't have a particular signal," Ms. Ellison said, "I just say, 'Mom, turn the page now.'") and served as her daughter's surrogate right hand, raising hers high when Ms. Ellison had something to say in class.

As a tribute, the mother received a mock degree in "virtual studies" from the seniors in her daughter's house.

"I'm the brawn," Mrs. Ellison said. "She's the brains."

The mother added that her daughter "can't understand what all the hoopla is about, which is refreshing."

Though she has never known the freedom of tossing a Frisbee across the Yard, Ms. Ellison insisted that hers had been a fairly typical Harvard existence. She has, for example, occasionally sipped a beer at Brew Moon in Harvard Square, though she has hardly made a habit of it.

"I'd be drinking and operating my wheelchair at the same time," she said. "That would classify me as DWI."

Ms. Ellison lived on campus all four years, studied with renowned professors such as Alan Dershowitz and Stephen Jay Gould, founded a student advocacy group on behalf of the disabled and attended her senior formal dance. But she is the first to say that her mother—as well as her father, younger brother and older sister—were only the starting lineup on a team deep in talent that made her graduation possible.

Her dormitory room was custom-fitted by Harvard technicians with a hospital bed, small hydraulic lift, panic button and electronic door opener. When she signed up for a class on the history of opera, it had to be moved because the building was inaccessible with a wheelchair.

And though she and her date stayed at the senior formal well past midnight, they had to be chaperoned by her mother (Ms. Ellison's brother, Reed, was his mother's escort) and were ferried from the party not in a white limousine but a white van with an open cargo bay.

Kevin Davis, a retired Cambridge police detective who would often drive Ms. Ellison to class, said: "Brooke's captured my heart. It's inspiring to know a person of her character."

Like one of her idols, the actor Christopher Reeve, who was paralyzed in a horseback riding accident, Ms. Ellison conceded that she does have moments of sadness, particularly when her sleep is interrupted by dreams of the dance classes that were her childhood passion. (A poster in her dorm room, brought from home, showed five pint-size ballerinas at a dance bar, the middle girl desperately trying to stretch to reach as high as the other four.)

She said she has never wanted to meet the man whose car hit her as she walked home from school, an accident that fractured her skull, her spine and almost every major bone in her body. But she said she holds no grudge.

"If I were to harbor anger for 10 years," she said, "it'd be too exhausting."

Even though she was a formidable student in high school who scored 1510 out of a possible 1600 on her College Board exams (she filled in the bubbles by dictating to a teacher), Ms. Ellison never expected to get into Harvard. "I thought if I got accepted, I would put the letter in a frame," she said.

But once she was admitted, she said, Harvard, which costs more than $30,000 a year, did everything they could to persuade her to attend. The university provided her with scholarships not only to supplement her father's salary as an administrator in a Social Security office but also to pay for her costly medical needs.

Now that she is graduating Ms. Ellison plans to spend a summer getting to know her family again and to write her autobiography. Eventually she hopes to travel as a motivational speaker.

"Anywhere people feel they need encouragement," she said, "that's where I hope to be."

Jacques Steinberg

Late for School

NEW PALTZ, N.Y.—Clara Miller's son-in-law drives her to school, carries her heavy book bag, steers her around patches of ice in the parking lot and runs interference in the stairwells where undergraduates push and shove.

Her back hurts most of the time. Her hearing is not good enough to sit in the back of a lecture hall unless the professor is using a microphone. She has had breast cancer and cataract surgery. She struggles to recall names and dates.

It's not easy being a 92-year-old college student.

Mrs. Miller is the oldest student in the State University of New York system and she is just 14 credits away from graduating with a degree in music. Still ahead is the dreaded science requirement, which she has put off, the same as many an 18-year-old. But if she can push through a heavy schedule next year, Mrs. Miller—white ringlets, stretch pants and all—could graduate alongside her 26-year-old granddaughter, Kristina Volberg.

"I used to say I got this far, so why should I bother going to college," said Mrs. Miller. "But everyone in my family but me had a college degree, and I didn't like that."

Mrs. Miller was telling her story from a rocking chair by the window in her apartment in Wappingers Falls, where a wall clock plays snippets of classical music every hour on the hour. Her schoolbooks are piled on a card table within easy reach. Her computer, linked to the university, is in the spare bedroom. Housecleaning has taken a back seat to her studies, she said, apologizing for the clutter.

She is able to go to college because of a program here that awards her course credit for experiences she's had during her life. Since she graduated from high school 75 years ago she has lived a lifetime filled with music—she has played and taught piano and organ, directed operettas, written church pageants and translated German cantatas. After reviewing all the musical work she has done, the college decided it was worth 88 credits. Students need 120 credits in order to graduate, so Mrs. Miller is taking classes to earn 32 more.

Teachers are impressed by Mrs. Miller. They say she brings years of knowledge to the classroom that the younger students do not have. One recent day, Mrs. Miller raised her hand to say that in her father's church, in the 1930's, women were barred from voting at congregational meetings, even if they were widowed and had no husband to represent them. She added that she was kept from applying to college, despite graduating at the top of her high school class, because her brother was in the seminary and her father could not afford to educate them both. Later she described a strict upbringing in which she had no choice but to become her father's organist at age 15.

Only after high school, when she traveled weekly to the Eastman School of Music in Rochester, did she find herself, Mrs. Miller said. There she studied piano under Ernst Bacon and organ under Abel Decaux, attended lectures by Ravel and Poulenc, went to opera rehearsals, tried her hand at conducting.

"It was the first freedom I felt in my life," she said.

Now she has found a different kind of freedom. Her 63-year-old son-in-law drives her to college every day, and drives from one parking lot to the next, as her class schedule requires, so Mrs. Miller doesn't have to walk too far. She appreciates this because it means she can leave her walking stick at home.

"Everybody tells me how spry I am," Mrs. Miller said. "I can't walk around here with a cane."

Jane Gross

ANOTHER DAY, ANOTHER 89 MILES TO SCHOOL

TERLINGUA, Tex.—The stars were still looming large in the West Texas sky when 14-year-old Joee Barnes devoured her corn flakes and ran for the door, grabbing her book bag, a blanket and a pillow. She was off in her father's car to catch the bus and head for school, 97 miles away. The time was 5:20 A.M.

It was another day and another trip to Alpine High School for Joee, her older brother, Charley, and 22 other teenagers from the Big Bend region along the Rio Grande. Their 89.7-mile trip to school takes about two hours each way—the longest daily school bus route in the United States. And some students have to travel 45 minutes more just to get to their bus stop, meaning they spend more time getting back and forth to school than they actual spend in their classroom.

Past Hen Egg, Packsaddle, Elephant, Cathedral and a dozen other desert mountain peaks, the bus lumbered, climbing 4,000 feet, as most students tried to doze. A few whispered to each other; some just stared out the window. At 7:40, the bus wheeled into Alpine.

"It's hard," said Joee when she returned home to Terlingua 13 hours after she had left, hungry for dinner. "It's hard to eat, do your homework and have a life, hanging out on the bus all day."

For students here in the southernmost part of Texas's biggest county, where there is far less than one person for every square mile of land, there is no local high school. The towns—Terlingua, Lajitas and Study Butte (pronounced STOO-dee byoot)—are too small and too poor to build one. The only way to get an education is to hop on the bus and head for Alpine.

It is a ride that has its consolations, especially for the bus driver, Melody Clarke, who is paid $27.50 each way, every trip. She stays in Alpine all day, running errands for people from Terlingua. The other day she bought some Christmas lights for one family, filled a pre-scription for another and made a deposit at the county's only bank for a third. For one thing, she really does get to watch the deer and the antelope play.

"We get some gorgeous sunrises and sunsets out here," she said, "and I get paid to watch every single one of them." Indeed, on the trip home the other day, the early evening sun lit up the mesas of the Texas high desert in spectacular shades of purple, red and brown.

But for most of the students, who quickly grow oblivious to the scenery, and for their parents, who rise every day long before dawn to make sure their children get off to school, it is an exhausting ordeal.

"It's just awfully long," said Jack Probst, the superintendent of the Terlingua School District, whose school stops at the eighth grade. "It's too dadgum long."

The students sleep on the bus, they socialize on the bus, a few even try to do their homework on the bus. "That doesn't really work, though," said Jo Ann Klingemann, a freshman from Terlingua. "You get nauseous. The teacher can't read it."

High school love has flared up and fizzled out on the bus, under the watchful eye of Mrs. Clarke and her husband, Robert, a retired deputy sheriff from the Houston area, who often comes along just to keep his wife company.

"Boys and girls may sit together, but they know the rules," said Mrs. Clarke, a jolly woman who sports wide pink glasses and a tie-dyed T-shirt. "I must be able to see both heads and all hands at all times."

And for many of the students, the bus has almost become an extension of their homes. "Some days, I just wake up as we come in to Alpine," said 17-year-old Charley Barnes, a junior. "I'm already on the bus, and I don't remember how I got here."

People here and in Lajitas and Study Butte, which together have a year-round population of barely 500, have certainly tossed around a lot of ideas about building a high school. One plan would have interactive video in the classroom, linking the students by television screen to teachers in Alpine.

But every time they look into the idea, they discover that it would cost much more than the poor communities can afford. And so, students ride the bus, just as they have for the past 20 years.

Almost all 350 students at Alpine High, not just the ones who ride the bus from Terlingua, are used to traveling long distances. The Fightin' Bucks basketball team rode a school bus 105 miles north to Pecos the other evening, lost the game by two points and returned home close to midnight. But students from the Terlingua area are different because they have to ride long distances every day. And because there is no late bus—the one bus arrives back in Terlingua at 5:40 P.M.—they miss out on extracurricular activities, like sports or cheerleading or band.

"I'd love to try out for track, but first I'd have to find a place to live" in Alpine, said Joee, dressed in a plaid shirt and fresh-faced even hours before dawn, her blond hair pulled back in a ponytail.

The students on the bus already joke about what they will tell their own children. "It's like those parents who say they walked to school five miles every day without any shoes or something," Charley Barnes said. "I'll say, 'You kids, stop your whining. I traveled to school hundreds of miles, through the jungle, 115 degrees outside.'"

Others are less dramatic. "I'll just always feel proud of myself that I made it," said 17-year-old Susy Garcia of Terlingua, a senior riding the bus for her fourth and final year. "I didn't give up. But when I go college, I know one thing. It'd be real nice to be able to walk to class."

Sam Howe Verhovek

A lot of things happened because of this article about the Alpine school bus ride. The end result was that a new high school was built in Alpine. Sam Verhovek wrote this a few months before that new school opened:

The fund-raising started a few weeks after an article in The New York Times described the students' daily journey. Kathy Killingsworth, the principal of the Terlingua School who is about to become the district's superintendent, said the district received several calls offering help, and residents decided to form the nonprofit Big Bend Educational Corporation.

As other articles appeared, more help came. A man who read about the bus ride in the *Dallas Morning News* donated 320 acres of land in West Texas, which the corporation sold for $18,000—"not exactly Manhattan prices, but it sure helped," said the Rev. Judith Burgess, vicar of the Big Bend Episcopal Mission, who heads the corporation.

The *National Enquirer* ran a story, and more contributions came in. A company in Ohio called to donate a septic system. A hardware store in Fort Stockton, Tex., donated the fencing. Altogether $148,000 was raised in cash and donated services, enough for a simple six-room Big Bend High School.

The district is still extremely poor, though it is growing, which should make a high school an increasingly sustainable proposition. The hamlets of Terlingua, Lajitas and Study Butte had populations of 25, 6 (yes, 6 people, total) and 120, respectively, in the 1980 census but now the communities have a combined year-round population of about 700, with much of the economy built around hikers, rafters and other tourists.

Now that the marathon here is over, there remains the question of which students in the country have the new longest bus ride. It seems there are school routes in both Wyoming and New Mexico that are around 75 miles long.

SPORTS

Riding to Fame and Fortune

Sports fans wait for certain history-making moments. In horse racing that moment comes when a horse wins first the Kentucky Derby, then the Preakness, and faces the final race in the Triple Crown—the Belmont Stakes. Very few horses even win the first two of these races. And far fewer win all three and take the crown—only 11 horses have ever done it.

The last horse to run for the crown was Funny Cide, a three-year-old gelding with a most unusual set of owners. Here is their story:

SACKETS HARBOR, N.Y.—Eight years ago on Memorial Day, after a weekend spent consuming several cases of beer, six old high school buddies, five businessmen and a teacher, sat on a porch and decided they needed something new and interesting in their lives.

They were certain of one thing: they had enjoyed the heck out of one another's company since the days in the 1960's, when they had played football and wore crew cuts at Sackets Harbor Central, the kindergarten–to–grade-12 school that still educates the children of this tiny village.

All these years later they call themselves the "Sackets Six" and they can't remember which one of them—was it Mark Phillips or his brother Pete?—came up with the idea to chip in and buy a horse. They agree, though, that it cost each of them $5,000 and that they began with simple goals: winning a race or two, maybe at the Saratoga racetrack.

Since that first horse, they have bought several others, though hardly enough to make them real players in the horse-racing world. Some of their horses have run well, but none has remarkably. At this moment, however, the Sackets Six own a horse that is poised to do the unthinkable. The star of their small barn, Funny Cide, captured the Kentucky Derby and the Preakness. With a victory in the Belmont Stakes, Funny Cide can become the 12th horse to win the Triple Crown.

"Not bad for some hicks from the sticks," J. P. Constance said, beaming in his easy chair at his home on Hounsfield Street, a mere eight furlongs from Lake Ontario. The Phillips brothers, Harold Cring and Larry Reinhardt laugh along with him as they have nearly every night the past two weeks while playing host to the dozens of camera crews and reporters who have trekked to this resort town 31 miles south of the Canadian border to ask how it feels to hit the lottery.

"It's a true blessing," said Mark Phillips, 55, a retired high school math teacher. He knows about these things: he has survived two bouts with cancer. "You got some guys who know absolutely nothing about horses; I'm just learning how to bet. And here we go and win the Derby and the Preakness and have a chance to bring home some history. This has been the ride of our lives."

Indeed, the crew possesses little horse sense, with the exception of the managing partner, Jack Knowlton, who like Mr. Reinhardt and Mark Phillips is a member of Sackets Harbor Central's Class of '65. He is the only member of the group who actually owned a horse before this partnership, and he is the primary investor in Funny Cide, owning 20 percent while his five childhood buddies own 4 per-

cent each. Four other investors—not friends, just business partners—own the remaining 60 percent. The smallest investors knew so
little when they began that Pete Phillips, a retired utility worker,
believed that Sackatoga Stable—the name for the partnership that
Mr. Knowlton created for the group—was an actual place, and that
his horses were kept there when they were not racing.

The smallest investors were also most surprised when Funny Cide
began showing potential greatness. Last fall he was scheduled to go
to Houston for a race that could have earned his owners $275,000.
The horse's trainer, Barclay Tagg, was against the idea, and thought
Funny Cide needed to rest until spring. He sent a message to the
partners that racing the horse in Houston might compromise his
chances of reaching the Kentucky Derby.

The partners thought that Mr. Tagg was out of his mind. "I was,
like, the Kentucky Derby, that's pie in the sky," said Pete Phillips,
who thought that resting the horse was simply throwing away a shot
at $275,000. But as it happened, Funny Cide came down with a
throat infection and was too sick to race. And those investors were
even more surprised still a few weeks before the Kentucky Derby,
when it seemed almost certain that Funny Cide would in fact qualify
for that race. Some Las Vegas casinos allow gamblers to place bets on
that race well before the actual competitors are chosen. The good
news for those gamblers is that the payoff on a well-placed bet is
higher. But the bad news is that if the horse turns out not to qualify
for the race at all, no one offers them their money back.

Mr. Knowlton explained this to his partners and told them that
he was flying to Las Vegas to place some bets. He collected their
money, but it turns out they had misunderstood what they were betting on. "I thought Jack said we were betting on Funny Cide to be
'in' the Kentucky Derby and I thought, well, that is not too much of
a stretch," Mr. Constance said. "When I got back the tickets and saw
the bet was to *win*, I almost fainted."

Funny Cide did win, of course, and those tickets paid more than
$100,000. But each and every one of the Sackets Six insists that nei-
ther the last eight years nor the past few weeks have been about
money. Funny Cide has already earned nearly $2 million. There is

another $1 million purse available at the Belmont, and a $5 million bonus waiting if he sweeps the Triple Crown, but for the partners the smaller moments they have already experienced are what they will treasure most.

For Mark Phillips, it is the tears that ran down his cheeks in the winner's circle at Churchill Downs and the realization that the moment was priceless. For Mr. Cring, it is the post-race celebration after the Preakness, where the Pimlico Race Course bugler played "New York, New York" and then a hundred friends and family from this tiny village belted out the alma mater of Sackets Harbor Central. For Mr. Reinhardt and Pete Phillips, it is the scores of cards and letters they receive from neighbors and strangers who are enthralled that something good could happen to a bunch of regular guys who go to work every day. For Mr. Constance, it is those triumphant rides home from Churchill Downs and Pimlico aboard a yellow school bus, with his oldest friends all still enjoying the heck out of one other's company. They took a yellow school bus together to their first race, and now they take a yellow school bus to every race.

"You know, no matter what happens in the Belmont, we still got plenty in front of us," he said. "For all we've accomplished, we've yet to achieve what we set out to do: We haven't won a race at Saratoga yet."

Joe Drape

News of Funny Cide and his folksy, regular-guy owners had made news around the world by the day of the race. It poured the morning of the Belmont Stakes, and Joe Drape was there to watch what happened:

Instead of dousing the spirits of those who came to be part of history, the rain that pounded Belmont Park yesterday afternoon made their hope blossom. This was Funny Cide's home track. He was New York–born and had captured two-thirds of the Triple Crown. A little slop? Forget about it. His last five workouts at Belmont had been the fastest of the day—two in conditions as soupy as these. The track was sticky three weeks earlier at the Preakness, and Funny Cide seemed to ski over the mud. So what if rain pounded the 135th running of the Belmont Stakes? Funny Cide was going to pound his five rivals.

At least that was the feeling in the North Shore Terrace, the dining room where J. P. Constance was probably the only optician in the world signing autographs. A Funny Cide victory was the desperate wish of the soaked crowd of 101,864.

All those hopes and wishes went unfulfilled. Like War Emblem, Charismatic, Real Quiet and Silver Charm in the past seven years, Funny Cide could not win the Belmont and capture the Triple Crown. He finished third behind Empire Maker and the runner-up, Ten Most Wanted.

Until Funny Cide, a chestnut gelding who was the even-money favorite, broke from the gate, this was among the finest miserable days in New York history. And then?

Nothing really went wrong in Funny Cide's bid to become the 12th Triple Crown champion, a feat that horseplayers have been waiting to celebrate since 1978, when Affirmed won the Belmont. It was just that nothing really went right, either.

"We were beaten by a good horse," said Mr. Tagg, Funny Cide's stoic and straightforward trainer. "I don't know what else to say. I am being honest. It is horse racing."

His jockey, Jose Santos, started Funny Cide fast out of the gate, just as he did in the Kentucky Derby and Preakness. Funny Cide glided like a hovercraft into the first turn, leaving Scrimshaw and Empire Maker in his wake. Santos and Funny Cide were loping at a sensible place—a half-mile in 48.70 seconds, three-quarters of a mile in a manageable 1:13.51.

From his vantage point in a clubhouse box, Mr. Tagg glanced up from beneath a brown fedora to the toteboard clocks. He felt pretty good.

"I was pretty confident when he made the three-quarter mark at 1:13 and change," he said. But from his seat a length behind Funny Cide, Jerry Bailey, the jockey riding Empire Maker, was seeing the best thing imaginable for his colt: Mr. Santos was asking, begging, fighting Funny Cide to slow down.

Heading into the far turn, Bailey knew that redemption for Empire Maker, for himself and for the colt's trainer, Bobby Frankel, was just a half-mile away. They had beaten Funny Cide in the Wood Memorial in April only to be embarrassed in the Derby, when Empire Maker was the heavy favorite. Now Bailey watched Santos wrestling with Funny Cide and turned his own colt loose.

"I knew I had him," Bailey said. "He couldn't get him to settle down."

So Bailey asked Empire Maker to run. As they entered the final stretch, Mr. Frankel, Empire Maker's trainer, watched and knew he had everyone's favorite horse beat. "But I still had an anxious moment with Ten Most Wanted," he said.

The jockey Pat Day had Ten Most Wanted, the Illinois Derby winner, in full stride, and his colt was pole-vaulting down the middle of the lane. Ten Most Wanted lunged and lurched, but came up three-quarters of a length short of Empire Maker.

Empire Maker finished in 2:28.26 and paid $6 on a $2 bet to win.

In the owners' box, the faces of Funny Side's owners, Mr. Santos's family and Mr. Tagg said that the five-week celebration of a modestly bred, cheaply purchased overachiever was through. Mr. Constance and Mr. Knowlton watched with watery eyes before giving respectful applause to Empire Maker. Rita Santos and her 8-year-old son, Jose Jr., collapsed tearfully into each other's arms. Mr. Tagg kept his usual stone face intact, although his squinted eyes betrayed his disappointment.

Maybe most broken-hearted of all were Funny Cide's legions of fans who had come to see a blue-collar horse, trained by an everyday trainer and owned by a group of regular guys, perhaps grab greatness.

"I feel bad for the people who were so behind him," Mr. Tagg said.

WOMEN'S SOCCER TAKES OFF

PASADENA, Calif.—They played to near collapse, through 120 minutes of soccer, 90 minutes of regulation melting into 30 minutes of overtime under a brutal sun, and still no one had put the ball into the net in the final of the Women's World Cup. And so the United States won soccer's world championship over China by the sport's most tense and capricious arbiter—penalty kicks. Five players from each team set the ball up 12 yards from goal in the penalty-kick phase, leaving the shooters and goalkeepers alone, one on one, to decide the match as much by chance as by skill. All a goalie can do is guess, act on instinct. If she guesses correctly, she is a hero. If not, there is no resistance to be offered, only a futile leap or a dive one way, while the ball flies unimpeded in the opposite direction.

The crowd of 90,185 was the largest to ever watch a women's sporting event in the United States—in the world, organizers believe. American Brandi Chastain's kick consummated three weeks

of unprecedented interest in a sport that filled huge arenas with soccer moms and dads and their daughters, who painted their faces red,
white and blue in star-spangled admiration of the American players.
Grownups finally began recognizing the sporting heroes their kids
had discovered long ago. Even President Clinton was in attendance
today, having been drawn into the swirl of popularity surrounding
the United States team. Perhaps gone forever is the myth that women's
sports cannot attract crowds and that the games that women play are
somehow lesser than the games men play. The Women's World Cup
will undoubtedly be remembered as an epochal moment in women's
sports, along with the Billie Jean King–Bobby Riggs tennis match in
1973, and the passage of Title IX in 1972, which essentially forbid
discrimination on the basis of gender.

Although many find penalty kicks an unsatisfying way to decide
a match—the 1994 men's World Cup was decided here the same
way—the victorious American women still made a forceful case for a
professional league of their own.

At the start of overtime, things did not look promising. America's most confident and accurate taker of penalty kicks, midfielder
Michelle Akers, had left woozily at the end of regulation play and
spent the rest of the game in the American locker room with heat
exhaustion.

Despite a career threatened by chronic fatigue syndrome, Akers
dominated today's game in defensive midfield, sliding ferociously,
sledgehammering teammates and opponents in her path and using
her head to catapult away one Chinese kick after another. She was
the first great star of this team, and Coach Tony DiCicco calls her
the greatest woman ever to play the game.

But Akers stopped a shot with her face near the end of regulation, then crumpled to the ground after heading away a corner kick,
no longer able to help her team.

With Akers gone, China began to attack forcefully and the
Americans seemed weary and vulnerable. Ten minutes into overtime, China's Liu Ying played a corner kick to teammate Fan Yunjie,
who flicked the ball with her head past the outstretched right arm of
Briana Scurry, the American goalie. But Kristine Lilly, the world's

most experienced player with 186 international appearances, stood exactly where she was supposed to, on the goal line, near the left post, and headed the ball away. Lilly was named the most valuable player of the game.

"Lill is a workhorse," Scurry said. "There's no one I would trust more on that post."

After a pair of 15-minute periods of scoreless overtime, the exhausted, drained American and Chinese players gulped bottles of water and lay on the turf as trainers massaged their aching, cramped muscles to help them prepare for the penalty kicks.

Xie Huilin stepped up first for China and punched a shot into the top left corner of the net. Carla Overbeck, the American captain, went to the right and pumped her fist with a celebratory skip down-field. Qiu Haiyan of China placed a ball just beyond Scurry's reach, then Joy Fawcett did a stutter step and slotted the ball into the right corner, tying the penalty kicks at 2–2.

Liu Ying was next up for China, but she seemed hesitant and exposed her intentions, and Scurry dived to her left, punching the ball away with both hands.

Scurry has been in some nail-biting games, but no save of hers was more important or dramatic than this one.

"I knew all I had to do was to stop one, and we'd probably win it," Scurry said. "She hit it hard, but she didn't place it that well."

Lilly then put a left-footed shot into the net, and the Americans were up by 3–2. Zhang Ouying tied it right up.

Mia Hamm, who did not score in her fourth consecutive game through overtime, and who has admitted to lacking confidence on penalty kicks, made an assured move this time, putting the Americans up, 4–3, and jumping relievedly into the arms of her teammates.

Sun Wen, the Chinese captain who was tied for the leading scorer in the tournament with seven goals, was up next for China. She had been shut down by Akers in midfield and by Overbeck and Kate Sobrero on the back line, but this time Sun shot precisely inside the left post to equalize the penalty-kick phase at 4–4.

Now it was Brandi Chastain's turn. If she made the shot, the Americans would win. If she didn't, a new round of penalty kicks would begin. She had banged a right-footed penalty kick off the crossbar against China in a 2–1 loss in February at a tournament in Portugal, but Coach Tony DiCicco called on her again today, and Chastain curled a left-footer into the upper right corner. There was nothing that China's goalkeeper, Gao Hong, could do, and the tired Americans had won.

"Being fifth, there's a lot of pressure," Chastain said. "But my teammates trusted me. I had been practicing all week and I felt very confident."

Her confidence found its mark. She kicked that final and decisive ball inside the right post. Then Chastain—the player nicknamed "Hollywood" for her theatricality—whipped off her jersey, twirling it like a lariat over her head. The crowd erupted in celebration and confetti cannons dusted the field as Chastain was engulfed by her teammates, who had been linked arm in arm at midfield, bending over, hoping, maybe even praying, for the winning kick.

"Momentary insanity," Chastain said of her celebration. "I thought, 'This is the greatest moment of my career,' and I lost control."

Jere Longman

HOW OLD IS DANNY ALMONTE?

New Yorkers were abuzz all summer over one Bronx Little League Team, the Rolando Paulino All-Stars. The team was only the fourth one from New York, and the first from outside Staten Island, ever to make it to the Little League World Series. The teams roster was an embodiment of the American Dream—although all but one of the players were born in New York, their families all came from Puerto Rico and the Dominican Republic. They grew up practicing baseball in weed-infested patches of city parks. This season, a Wall Street firm donated $50,000 to sponsor the team; but before that the players relied on neighborhood bodegas to help them pay for uniforms and equipment.

At the World Series, the team was followed around by a growing contingent of fans, sportswriters and camera crews. The main reason for all this attention was their star pitcher, Danny Almonte, who had come from the Dominican Republic two years earlier with his father, Felipe, and who still struggled to speak English. Early in the series Danny pitched a no-hitter and a perfect game—the first perfect game in a Little League World Series for nearly 50 years. His pitches were as fast as 70 miles per hour.

Not bad for a 12-year-old. But was Danny really 12 years old? Members of competing teams didn't think so, and even paid a detective $10,000 to prove them right. He came up empty-handed. League officials asked again and again to see the original of Danny's birth certificate. They declared themselves satisfied that he was really 12.

This is the profile of Danny that ran the morning of the big game, the game that would qualify the team for the semi-final round, the game that would determine the United States Championship.

WILLAMSPORT, Penn.—The boys stepped up to home plate on the dirt diamond in the small Dominican town of Moca, broomsticks in their hands. But the pitches came so fast that many of them flinched and jumped back. The objects burst out of 9-year-old Danny Almonte's left hand like satellites flung out of orbit. He threw ragged baseballs, or tiny metal rings stripped off milk bottles, or whatever could be scavenged.

Danny's father tried to keep his jaw from dropping while watching this day after day. He had never taught his son how to throw curveballs or sliders for fear of damaging Danny's arm. But his son was making it look as effortless as breathing.

Felipe Almonte decided then that Danny would have to play boys a year or two older than his son. "It's like he's been playing ball since he was born," Almonte said here today. "He would fire the ball in too hard."

At 12, Danny now plays in the United States, but he is no less a prodigy. "I don't know if anyone's ever seen a 12-year-old throw the ball like he throws it," said Bob Brewer, manager of the team the All-Stars will face tonight. "He doesn't seem to get rattled by anything that goes on."

Because there are so many questions about Danny's real age,

Rolando Paulino, the Bronx league's president, brought out his players' passports and birth certificates. He unfolded Danny Almonte's and said it was the original.

Written in Spanish, with a single brown stamp on the front and three on the back, it certified that Danny was born on April 7, 1989, to Sonia Rojas.

Lance Van Auken, a Little League spokesman, said the Rolando Paulino team had been thoroughly checked by officials at each level of tournament play.

The district administrator saw their original birth certificates and passports and gave them an affidavit certifying their eligibility, Van Auken said. This was much more than most Little League teams have to do—the usual requirement is simply to present the affidavit as they move up the tournament ladder. But because the Bronx team has been challenged so many times, officials at the highest levels have personally looked at the original documents.

Back in the village of Moca, Danny's mother has applied for a visa to travel to the United States to see her son play. She is turning 28 on Saturday, and American consulate officials in Santo Domingo told her that she seemed too young to be Danny's mother. They asked to see a copy of his birth certificate, she said. Her brother obtained one today from Jamao, a village near Moca. Then, she said, the officials asked to see the original. She did not have it, she said, it was in Williamsport, with Danny.

Edward Wong

Danny Almonte did not pitch the night of the U.S. Championship game, because the rules say the same pitcher cannot pitch two games in a row. Almonte played center field, instead, and eight busloads of fans from the Bronx filled the bleachers. American and Dominican flags fluttered in their hands, and the fans rose to their feet when the Bronx players entered the dugout before the game.

This is what happened:

Some of the baby Bronx Bombers, as they have come to be known, said it was the best vacation of their lives. They had gorged themselves on pizza, flirted with girls and made friends from other countries. They had learned how to say "baseball" in a handful of languages. Better yet, they had played ball and played it well in the Little League World Series.

But their seemingly endless summer came to a close today.

In the biggest game of their lives, the Rolando Paulino All-Stars from the Bronx lost by 8–2 to the team from Apopka, Florida. Before thousands of people at the Howard J. Lamade Stadium, Apopka's Brandon Brewer, a 4-foot-10-inch, 81-pound shortstop, hit a three-run home run to right-center field off the first pitch he saw from Luilly Vinas in the top of the third inning. The next inning, Tyler Scanlon hit a three-run shot, putting the Florida team ahead by 6–1. Rolando Torres relieved Vinas in the fifth, but Apopka scored two more runs, one on a sacrifice fly by Andrew Cobb and one on a fielding error, putting Florida ahead, 8–1.

The Bronx team opened the scoring in the first inning when Torres scored on a wild pitch by Stuart Tapley, who had 12 strikeouts and was the winning pitcher. The Bronx team's final run came in the fifth when Reynaldo Guava sprinted home after another wild pitch. To fire up the team, hundreds of Bronx fans rose to their feet, pounded drums and chanted, but the game had already been decided. Apopka had six hits to the Bronx's four, and it will go on to play Japan on Sunday evening for the Little League World Series title.

Players from the Bronx and Apopka embraced after the game even as some of the Baby Bombers fought back tears. "We win, we lose, they did the best they could," Manager Alberto Gonzalez of the Bronx team said. "This is the way we are. This is the way we'll always be."

Ken Tapley, an Apopka coach, said he "couldn't have been prouder to play them in the final game."

"It's tremendous for the Bronx and for New York City," Mayor Rudolph W. Giuliani, wearing sunglasses and a blue cap, said minutes after taking his seat. "It's great for the kids, and really, it's captured the imagination of New York City."

"No matter if they lost, they played a good game," said Pedro Garcia, the uncle of left fielder Carlos Garcia. "There's nothing you can take away from them."

The Rolando Paulino players will be given keys to the city by Mayor Giuliani and honored in a parade in the Bronx next week. After today's game, many of the players tried to wind down, hugging their families and signing baseballs for fans on a hill overlooking the stadium. A half-moon climbed into the sky as the sun slipped away.

"I feel great that I had a challenge with that team, but today wasn't our day," third baseman Hector Rodriguez said.

Then a security guard came around and told the players that dinner was ready. They raced off, remembering that their coaches had promised them pizza. Maybe summer still had a few hours left.

Their season was over, but the questions didn't go away. A reporter from Sports Illustrated *magazine presented Little League officials with a document signed by a government official in Moca saying that a boy named Danny Almonte was born April 7, 1987—not 1989 as his father had said. That would make him 14 years old, which is too old to play Little League ball. An official investigation was begun. Reporter Ed Wong, who watched Danny play in the World Series, wrote the following:*

"I think for us at this point, what we have are conflicting documents," Van Auken said. "As far as we're concerned, we're still considering the team as having been eligible and finished third in the tournament. I would say we're probably going to look into this further and take any action that might be appropriate once we find out what the truth is.

"I don't think anybody has proven to us that Danny Almonte is not eligible."

According to *Sports Illustrated,* which released an article last night based on its findings, Almonte's father, Felipe, registered his son's birth twice—once in December 1994 in Moca, when he submitted the birthday as April 7, 1987, and again in March 2000 in

Santo Domingo, when he submitted the birthday as April 7, 1989. The conflicting dates are recorded in separate books in the two cities, the article said. Parents in the Dominican Republic sometimes wait years to register their children's births. The 1989 date was recorded shortly before Danny Almonte joined his father in the Bronx, where Felipe works as a clerk in a bodega.

In each of the books, Felipe Almonte had also recorded his name and the name of Danny's mother, Sonia Margarita Rojas Breton, a 28-year-old native of Moca who no longer lives with him. The entries also had the personal identification numbers—similar to Social Security numbers in this country—for both parents, and they were the same in the two books, according to the *Sports Illustrated* article. That would mean that the same Danny Almonte was recorded in each book.

Paulino, the head of the Bronx team, said yesterday that his documents show Almonte to be 12. He said he faxed to the Little League yesterday copies of Almonte's passport, visa and a government affidavit from the Dominican Republic certifying that Almonte's birthday is April 7, 1989. Those original documents were provided to the league by Felipe Almonte, Paulino said.

"For me, it's O.K. because I have the documents," Paulino said. "I have the documents that Danny's father gave to us."

One of those documents, which Paulino showed reporters, was a piece of paper typed in Spanish. It was signed by a government official and had a single brown stamp on the front and three brown-and-green ones on the back. It said that a boy named Danny de Jesus was born to Sonia Rojas on April 7, 1989. That piece of paper and the one obtained by the *Sports Illustrated* reporter looked essentially the same—except for the birth year and possibly the name of the government official.

While officials investigated, Danny and his teammates celebrated.

As the Rolando Paulino All-Stars received glittering keys to New York yesterday from Mayor Rudolph W. Giuliani on the steps of City

Hall, the Dominican government started an investigation into why there are apparently two conflicting birth records for the team's ace pitcher, Danny Almonte.

The controversy over whether Almonte is 12 or 14 years old and eligible to play in the Little League was never mentioned during the noontime festivities for the Baby Bronx Bombers. But it hung unspoken in the air, clinging to the celebration that took place in front of roughly 300 fans, friends and family members. As 13 of the Rolando Paulino players sat in red team T-shirts and caps on a makeshift stage, politicians and businessmen stood up one after the other to give them plaques, gift certificates and handshakes, never once alluding to the issue on many people's minds.

"It's wonderful to be here with another team from the Bronx who distinguished themselves so well," Giuliani said, referring to the World Champion New York Yankees. "This team brought not only the entire Bronx together, but the entire city together."

When Almonte quietly walked up to receive his key to the city, the mayor slipped an arm around the lanky pitcher and smiled for photographers.

He later said at a news conference inside City Hall that "the young man and all the young men should be given the benefit of the doubt."

The players took a tour on the floor of the New York Stock Exchange in the afternoon and rang the closing bell there at 4:30. They then scrambled aboard a bus to the ESPN Zone restaurant in Times Square. There, some of them signed T-shirts while others stared at a silent television news broadcast about the questions over Almonte's age.

"My child couldn't sleep last night because of this," said Carmen Valles, the mother of the player Christopher Geronimo. "He had a headache all evening, just concerned and saying, 'Why are they doing this to us?'"

Reporter Joyce Wadler went to the Bronx to see whether the controversy was souring Danny's fans:

On the streets of the pitcher's home borough (O.K., adopted home borough), he is viewed as a hero, and the matter of when he was born was seen as mere nitpicking about statistics.

People lined up five deep along the Grand Concourse screaming for the team, especially for the tall, shy pitcher on the team's float. There were signs supporting him—"Whether 12 or 14 years of age, your performance motivated our kids, thanks Danny!" There were other placards in the predominantly Latino crowd claiming that the questions raised about Danny's age were motivated by racism—"Why investigate only us? Why? Because we're from the Bronx."

Even those people who spoke little English, like Mayra Trujillo, who comes from Cuba and lives on the Grand Concourse, had mastered the words that mattered on the big day.

"April 7, '89," Mrs. Trujillo said in English, repeating one of the two birth dates for Danny that have been in the news of late, after a long, passionate defense of the pitcher in Spanish. "No '87."

Who wants to give up a hero? Particularly when he is an immigrant in a borough of newcomers. Danny, who was not seen speaking to reporters, appeared to hold himself back from the crowd, even as a teenage girl was seen slipping him her phone number. On the team float, he stood close to Mr. Paulino, who put his arm around Danny and kept it there. With the other hand, Mr. Paulino occasionally blew kisses to the crowd.

There were some who had concerns about Danny, as the parade, with salsa dancers and other proud and excited Bronx Little Leaguers, made its way from 165th Street to the Bronx Courthouse.

Louis Rivera, 40, a sun-umbrella salesman who lives on Laconia Avenue and was attending the parade "to see the kids and make a few bucks," admitted that if Danny was 14, he would be upset.

"It would be kind of rough on the kids who lost," Mr. Rivera said. "When they put the other pitcher in, the other teams were getting runs. It's not fair. Those kids could have had a fighting chance."

Belkis Garcia, a legal secretary from the Bronx, who had come to the parade with a half-dozen relatives, including her two sons, saw it differently. "We're proud of what these kids had accomplished; kids from the South Bronx who made it as far as they did," Mrs. Garcia said. She called the controversy over Danny's age "very bad timing."

"I blame the media," she said. "There were also persons who got paid thousands of dollars to investigate the genuineness of the birth certificates of kids from the Bronx. Let's investigate kids from other areas. There were kids who looked older than 12 years to me."

At the Bronx Courthouse, a chant ran through the crowd as the Bombers, flanked by their coaches and the costumed Universal Studios characters Beetlejuice and Shrek took the top of the steps.

"Danny, tranquilo, el pueblo esta contigo," the crowd sang, meaning, "Danny, stay calm, the people are with you."

There were speeches; there was a press agent handing out leaflets to the reporters about Universal Orlando treating the team to a four-day trip to its resort in Florida. There was a salsa singer and female salsa dancers in slit silver skirts and, toward the end of the celebration, an invitation that the team's players and the girls dance. Many of the boys kept their distance, sticking together, acting like 12-year-olds, but a few danced with the girls, some displaying fine moves. And in front of the courthouse, a world away from the allegations and investigations, the village danced with them.

About a week after the controversy began, it ended. Officials of the Dominican Republic ruled that the second of the boy's birth certificates was fake, and that he was 14, not 12. That meant he was ineligible to play in Little League the last two seasons. As a result, Little League officials stripped the team of all its victories this season and began an investigation into the management of the Rolando Paulino Little League. And it barred Paulino and Danny's father, Felipe Almonte, "from any further association or involvement with the Little League program worldwide."

No one blamed Danny. They blamed the adult who took advantage of him. New York Mayor Giuliani said the misrepresentation "sadly hurts all the dedicated young boys who played their hearts out throughout the season and postseason play. The city has no intention of asking that the keys to the city be returned. It would only add to the hurt and pain that the innocent children of this team are already experiencing. Hopefully, all those involved will learn a valuable lesson about the importance of honesty and integrity in sports."

And President George W. Bush, a member of the Little League Hall of Excellence, said: "I'm disappointed that adults would fudge the boy's age," he said. "I wasn't disappointed in his fastball and his slider. The guy is awesome; he's a great pitcher. But I was sorely disappointed that people felt like they could send in a false age."

It was also learned that although Danny had been in the United States for nearly two years, his father had never enrolled him in school, a situation that some people found even more upsetting than the false birth certificate.

At the Frozen Ropes batting cages in New Rochelle, N.Y., Jamal Wright stood placidly outside one of the cages, balls thumping the canvas behind him, as he talked frankly about what he saw as the Big Betrayal.

"When I watched him, I thought he looked like he was 12, but he might have been hunched over," said Jamal, who is 10 and was waiting his turn to swat balls hurled out of a machine at 45 miles an hour. "Then when I heard, I couldn't believe it. It was bad what he did. Real bad. I sure wouldn't want to be him when I got home."

From city parks in Brooklyn and the Bronx to suburban batting cages like Frozen Ropes (named after baseball lingo for a line drive), young tongues were wagging pretty steadily yesterday. "I was sitting and watching TV and I heard it," Jamal said. "I went to my room and took down all the baseball pictures and put up basketball players. I was mad. He shouldn't have done that."

Among youngsters who in fanciful daydreams might envision themselves mowing down batters on television, there was a mixture of anger, rebuke, sadness, embarrassment and, in a few cases, heartfelt forgiveness. ("Like, not all kids know exactly how old they are," one young boy said.)

Some of the ballplayers, speaking in disconnected conversations during one of the final lazy days of summer break, wanted him suitably punished. A few thought cheating and lying were childhood habits that could be excused, especially since Danny obviously liked baseball so much and, on TV at least, seemed like a nice enough kid.

The majority of the youngsters, though, had zealously rooted for the Baby Bombers, their own emotions churning with the team's successes and failures, and they felt cheated by the ugly ending.

"I liked him when he was doing well; I think we all did," said Orrin Stancil, 11, of Brooklyn. "But now that all this has come out, I think he's a sham."

Malcolm Eggleston, 12, also of Brooklyn, was miffed, too: "If he's 14, why should he be playing in the little man's game? I don't think he deserves any of the recognition he gets."

At the sandlot baseball diamond in Highbridge Park in the Dominican enclave of Washington Heights, the crowd of young ballplayers felt the incident was an embarrassment and affront to the city. "I was proud when Danny was striking people out," said Luis Almanzar, 12. "Now I'm disappointed."

A contingent of kids from the Bronx on an outing with the Goodwill Baptist Church arrived at Frozen Ropes in the early afternoon. Some of them brought a different perspective to the issue than Little League officials were likely to.

Allen Gouldborne, 13, smacked a couple of terrific shots, then stepped out of the cage. He said he felt that age precision was overrated. "I mean, if the teams are for kids, I think 14 is still a kid, so they should let him play," he said. "Even though he lied, I don't know if he knew there was an age limit."

Thomas Goodwin, 17, who was standing nearby and eavesdropping, rolled his eyes. "Give me a break," he said.

Allen had other defenses to offer: "Well, at least he's not doing something else with his time, like roaming the streets or doing drugs."

Then he said, "And everybody lies."

About what?

"Everything. It's not like everyone's perfect. Say I batted in the cage, and nobody was watching, and I missed it. I could say, 'Hey, I hit it.' This stuff happens, you know."

Orenzo Harrell, 10, picked up on that theme. "Like kids are talking in class and they say, 'No, I didn't talk,' " he said. "Sometimes in school I'm in the chair and I get out of the chair to talk and the teacher says, 'Did you get out of the chair?' and I say, 'No.' But what he did was a big lie."

Was he mad at Danny?

"No, I'm not that mad," he said. "I just don't want him to get into trouble, because he looks like a nice kid."

Charles Platt, 13, who lives in New Rochelle, said that Danny was wrong but that he could understand his motivation. That was his team, "and he didn't want to leave it because he didn't want to leave his friends."

Though many of the youths were shocked by the confirmation of Danny's age, some said they had doubts about Danny early on.

Thomas Goodwin, who pitches for his own Bronx team, figured that something was fishy when he learned about the speed of Danny Almonte's fastball. "I don't know a 12-year-old kid with a 74-mile-an-hour fastball," he said. "I just got up to 80, and I'm 17. I was at 40 or 50 miles an hour when I was 12. I thought he was older, but my friends didn't believe me. Now they believe me."

Steven Valdez, 12, a pudgy pitcher from Washington Heights, said: "He has a curveball, and I can't throw one. My father said it would make my arm swollen."

Kids were divided on what ought to happen next, especially since some said that they felt that the parents were to blame and that maybe Danny Almonte didn't actually know he wasn't 12.

"I think he just found out when we found out," said Joseph Tulloch, 13, who is from the Bronx. If he did know, Thomas Goodwin said, Danny ought to be deported to his native Dominican Republic. Others concluded that it was enough if he was just yelled at pretty harshly or had to miss dinner for a few evenings. Stanley Diaz, 10, who was warming the bench in Highbridge Park, said: "He cheated. He lied. That's wrong. Now he should give that key back to the mayor."

This is not, of course, an exclusively boy issue. Melissa Fernandez, 14, and her sister, Adriene, 15, were watching the batting at

Frozen Ropes, though they had no intention of giving it a try. "The balls are flying too fast," Adriene pointed out. They both agreed that Danny Almonte was in hot water, but they said that they felt the context was important.

"Just put him on another team," Adriene said. "It's not that serious."

"Yeah, it's bad, but it's not awful," Melissa said.

What would be awful?

"If he killed somebody to get on the team," Melissa said.

"Or threatened to kill somebody to get on the team," Adriene said.

"Right," Melissa said. "That would really be awful. But even adults lie about their age."

"A lot," Adriene said.

N. R. Kleinfield

Focusing on the Olympics

EUGENE, Ore.—Her boyfriend downloaded an article about her first road race and handed the printout to Marla Runyan in their tiny apartment with the Olympic rings on the living room wall. She placed the story in a magnifying device and scanned the paragraphs, knowing that somewhere it would prominently be mentioned that her vision was severely impaired.

"There it is, 'the legally blind runner,'" the 31-year-old Runyan said. "At least it's not in the headline."

Runyan suffers from a degenerative condition of the retina called Stargardt's disease, which has left her with a hole in the center of her vision. She has 20–300 vision in one eye, 20–400 in the other. She cannot see the tape at the finish line of the metric mile. She cannot read a stopwatch or watch a replay of her races without placing her face several inches from the television. She wears contacts and can see the track beneath her feet with peripheral vision, but her competitors are visible to her as shards of color and smudged faces and gauzy hairstyles.

Despite her impairment, Runyan has an encouraging chance at the Olympic track and field trials a few months from now, to become the first legally blind athlete to make an American team for the Winter or Summer Games. She has a chance to make the team at 800 meters, 1,500 meters or 5,000 meters. Runyan began running the 1,500 meters only last year but posted a personal best of 4 minutes 5.27 seconds; anything under 4 minutes is considered a very fast time, and only three runners in the world broke the 4-minute mark last year. She holds a number of records, and has placed high in the national championships, the Pan American Games, and the world championships.

In other words, Runyan's career is remarkable for many reasons beyond her visual impairment, and there is a hint of impatience and deflection in her voice when the subject of her eyesight arises, because such talk inevitably centers on limitation instead of possibility. She is restless for the day when someone will write about her as an athlete, not as a legally blind athlete.

"I would never say that if it wasn't for Stargardt's, I could run three seconds faster," Runyan said. "To me, it's not true. I should be prepared and experienced enough that it isn't going to be a factor. If I break a national record, maybe they will stop writing about my eyes. It's a matter of commitment. Some people have a bad attitude, and that's their disability."

She looks slightly to the side when she speaks, seeing with her peripheral vision, and she prefers to talk about what is possible, not impossible. She had an epiphany stepping onto the track at the world championships in Seville, she said. Even with her sooty vision, she was struck by the fractured beauty of the moment, the rim of the stadium with its hanging flags, the splendid flashes of color, the brightness and crispness of the track.

"I knew I could never go back to a regular life," Runyan said. "Things would never be the same. I know it's strange for someone with 20–400 vision to say everything looked clear, but it was so magnified that it seemed clear to me. I couldn't distinguish individual things, but I could see bright, magnificent colors. Colors seemed to stand out more than ever before."

At the Summer Olympics in Sydney, Australia, the stadium will be even bigger, the colors just as riotous. Certainly, the news media coverage will be more extensive than when Trischa Zorn, a visually impaired swimmer, narrowly failed to qualify for the boycotted 1980 Moscow Olympics, and when Jim Mastro served as an alternate on the wrestling team at the 1976 Montreal Olympics. So, the inspiration that Runyan provides as a legally blind elite athlete is incalculable, said Charlie Huebner, executive director of the United States Association for Blind Athletes. "All young blind kids aren't being told they can dream about something," Huebner said. "Marla is a huge role model. 'I can go to college, I can be a teacher, I can be a world-class athlete.' If you have high expectations, anything is possible."

Since her vision began to deteriorate when she was 9 and living in Camarillo, Calif., she has succeeded by refusing to live a life of lowered expectations. When she could no longer see well enough, at age 14, to follow a soccer ball, she switched to track and field and set a school record in the high jump at 5 feet 7 inches. At San Diego State University, Runyan competed not in one event, but in seven, the heptathlon. When she could not see the hurdles in front of her, she learned to jump by counting steps between the hurdles. Her coach taped playing cards to the hurdles to teach her to clear them by only a slight margin. Sometimes she used reflective tape to help her locate the high-jump bar and a tape measure to precisely calibrate her approach.

She excelled in the classroom as well as on the track. Her mother, Valerie Runyan, painstakingly wrote out enlarged versions of her reading material in high school. With the help of a magnifying device attached to a pair of glasses, she could read large-print books. She used visual-aid devices, audio books and assistants who read to her in college, graduating cum laude in 1991, then earning a master's degree in education of the handicapped. She learned to water-ski and scuba dive, and she was able to get her California driver's license with the help of a telescopic magnifying lens; she is not allowed to drive in Oregon.

"She has put herself through a lot of pain and suffering not to fail," said her father, Gary Runyan. "I think a lot of it is driven by a lack of vision and still wanting to succeed in spite of it. The biggest thing her mother and I did was not to set up any artificial barriers for Marla. We let her find her own barriers. Some she found painfully. But she also found the things she could do." What she is doing now is focusing on the Olympic trials. She has a ravenous appetite for information, using a screen enlarger on her computer to surf the Web, or having her boyfriend, Matt Lonergan, a former college runner, read newspapers and magazines to her. She sits a few inches from the television and together they watch the videotaped races of great runners.

Her own stride is beautifully strong and fluid, but, of course, there are inevitable small complications for any runner who is legally blind. She is bothered by the sun, especially in late afternoon. She relies on the cluster of officials and timing devices, seeing them out of the corner of her eye, to gauge the finish line. Because she cannot see her competitor's faces, or read their numbers, she takes her cues from their styles of running. And she has a tendency to run slightly wide on the track, adding distance to her races, because she is not yet comfortable or confident enough with the jostling of the pack.

"She's got to be able to find herself in a position within a pack and be comfortable and not worry about it," Mike Manley, her coach, said. "That's all part of experience. What she's done so far in such a short time is incredible."

If the pack strings out, and she finds herself more than three or four seconds off the pace, Runyan can also struggle to find the leaders. In the final of the world championship, she found it difficult to anticipate the speeding up and slowing down that takes place in a tactical race. At one point, she ran up onto the shoulder of Svetlana Masterkova of Russia and Regina Jacobs of the United States, who would finish first and second, then she found herself being passed by other runners both on the inside and outside.

"I don't know if it was something visual I missed, or whether it was a lack of experience," Runyan said.

That's what this spring and summer are for. Experience. Gary

Runyan has begun to have dreams of his daughter in Sydney. "The joy I would feel for her would be overwhelming," he said. "The other day, I fell asleep watching something on TV, and I dreamed she was coming out of the tunnel in Sydney. She was the flag bearer for the United States. It seemed so real. It seemed like it almost happened. Maybe it can."

Jere Longman

Just after Jere Longman's article ran, Marla Runyan had an accident that threatened her Olympic dreams:

While training in Eugene, Ore., less than two months before the Olympic trials, Runyan jumped out of the way to avoid a youngster on a bike on a running trail. She twisted her left leg, injuring the ilio-tibial band of tissue that runs from the hip to the knee. She could not run on a track or a trail for five weeks, running in a pool instead, and it was not until the Saturday before the trials that she began to train again on dry land. Exhausted, she began dry-heaving after the preliminary round and limped off the track in a way that seemed to suggest she had no chance.

However, she is one of the country's most versatile and resourceful athletes, and it showed. She received treatment on her leg before stepping on the track today, and even though she was in pain, she positioned herself smartly for a final sprint to the tape, placing third which was all she needed to qualify.

"It's awesome," Runyan said of making the Olympic team. "I never really think of my vision as much as the media does. And I don't think my competitors do, either. I think my vision is just a circumstance that happened. I never looked at it as a barrier. I never said I wanted to be the first legally blind Olympian. I just wanted to be on an Olympic team, me, Marla."

A Long Overdue Apology

NEW YORK, N.Y.—Sixty years is a long time to wait. It was long enough for Evelyn Maisel Witkin to stew over the pain that New York University caused her in her senior year, long enough for her to write letters to administrators, to avoid reunions and to tell her story to her children, and then to her grandchildren.

She was one of seven students suspended for three months in March 1941 for standing up for what she still feels was a just cause: protesting the university's complicity in discrimination against black athletes. The university has never made amends to the students. Never, that is, until tonight, when N.Y.U. will honor the group known as the Bates Seven at an annual campus dinner for student athletes and also display photos and documents on the bigotry that led to the protest movement.

In 1940 and 1941, Ms. Witkin and six fellow students helped lead thousands of classmates in denouncing a little-known but widespread practice in college athletics known as the "gentlemen's agree-ment." If a game was scheduled between two schools and one of them objected to black athletes participating, the opposing team would keep the black players out of the contest.

Southern schools were usually, though not always, the ones who made the request, historians say, and many northern universities, from Harvard to Rutgers to the University of Michigan, complied.

But Ms. Witkin, a biology major, and other students took action when they learned in the fall of 1940 that Leonard Bates, a star full-back on the N.Y.U. football team, would not be allowed to play in a November game at the University of Missouri.

They began circulating petitions, wore buttons and picketed the university administration, chanting, "Bates must play!" It was at the time the largest protest against the gentlemen's agreements, and it took place nearly two decades before the start of the mass civil rights movement.

The university resisted. Not only did it comply with Missouri's request to leave Mr. Bates at home, but it also eventually retaliated against the students who protested, suspending seven of them when they objected to decisions by N.Y.U. to hold a basketball player and track stars out of subsequent athletic events.

Most of the seven eventually graduated, and they went on to become novelists, scientists and teachers. But in the six decades since, many of them have harbored bitter feelings toward the univer-sity, scars that are fading now that the school is recognizing them.

"I was very surprised because I had given up expecting anything to happen," said Ms. Witkin, who is 80. "Sixty years is a long time. But it's nice to know they're going to do something. It was something that meant a lot to us at the time."

The recognition is a result of a letter-writing campaign begun last year by Ms. Witkin, who became a professor of genetics at Rut-gers, and Donald Spivey, a history professor at the University of Miami. Jeffrey T. Sammons, a history professor at N.Y.U., also lob-bied administrators.

The university is not actually calling the recognition an apology, but rather a tribute to students who suffered for what they believed

in. John Beckman, an N.Y.U. spokesman, said the university decided
not to apologize for actions administrators took in 1940 and 1941
because "we can't put ourselves in their shoes, and we can't turn back
the hands of time.

"Fundamentally, what we want to do is embrace these members
of our community and hold them up as models of people who fight
for an important cause," he said. "I would call it an acknowledgment
of good work and courage shown by members of our community."

In addition to Ms. Witkin, the former students to be honored are
Anita Krieger Appleby, Jean Borstein Azulay, Mervyn Jones, Naomi
Bloom Rothschild, Robert Schoenfeld and Argyle Stoute. With the
possible exception of Mr. Stoute, whom the university could not
locate, all are still alive. Five of them will be attending the dinner,
and a friend will stand in for Mr. Jones, who lives in England and is
recovering from a minor stroke.

Ms. Rothschild, 80, said this is the first positive acknowledgment
that she has received for her activism. "When it happened, I got no
support from the school, no support from my family," she said. "For
all these years I felt slightly guilty that maybe I had done the wrong
thing. Now I maybe see that I didn't do anything wrong."

Six decades is long enough to blur memories, but many of the
seven students still recall that New York University in the fall of
1940 was a campus brimming with causes: pro-Communist rallies,
pacifist demonstrations, protests against fascism in Spain. One histo-
rian said it was then one of the most radical campuses in the country.
But it was the plight of a single athlete that galvanized the largest
student movement that year.

Students first learned of the university's decision to withdraw Mr.
Bates from the game at Missouri when several football players
showed up at a student council meeting to discuss the situation, said
Ms. Azulay, who was the council's vice president. For many, it was
the first time they had heard of a gentlemen's agreement.

Ms. Azulay and others quickly began circulating petitions. On
Oct. 18 about 2,000 students picketed the administration building,
and that was when "Bates must play!" became a rallying cry.

The concept of a gentlemen's agreement arose in the late 19th century, when schools in the South began playing universities in the Northeast, said Charles Martin, an assistant professor of history at the University of Texas at El Paso, who is writing a book on the history of discrimination in college sports. Many states in the South had laws prohibiting black athletes from competing alongside whites. The gentlemen's agreement was aimed at getting northern schools to follow that system when they played southern teams on the road and sometimes even at home.

"The northern schools would be gracious hosts and yield to the wishes of their southern opponents, not willing to embarrass them," Mr. Martin said.

Rutgers, for example, kept Paul Robeson, a star football player and later a prominent stage actor, from playing in at least one game, Mr. Martin said. Harvard did the same with a lacrosse player, he said. In 1939 Boston College agreed to withdraw its star running back from the Cotton Bowl after the bowl committee and B.C.'s opponent, Clemson University, objected to his participation, Mr. Spivey said. As for Mr. Bates, the students at N.Y.U. gathered more than 4,000 signatures in his support. But the football team left the train station on Oct. 31, 1940, without him. It lost to Missouri, 33–0.

Students rallied again after hearing that Jim Coward, a black basketball player at N.Y.U., was barred from the team. The uproar continued in February 1941 when students learned that three black runners would be kept out of a track meet against Catholic University. The facts in those cases are still in dispute.

The following month, a dean and a faculty committee suspended the seven students for three months for circulating a petition without permission.

They were juniors or seniors, and some had to take summer classes to graduate in the fall. Mr. Stoute never got a degree, nor did Mr. Jones, who returned home to England to fight in World War II. "I would call it a very happy occasion," Mr. Jones, 79, said of tonight's tribute from his home in England. "It's good to know that things do move on."

After World War II, many universities, including N.Y.U, began dropping the gentlemen's agreement as pressure from students and politicians mounted.

"This brings attention to a most important but seemingly under-represented, little-known chapter in collegiate athletics," Mr. Sammons, the N.Y.U. history professor, said. "Sometimes, sport can, instead of challenging what is discriminatory, contribute to it and make it stronger, at the expense of fair play." The dinner tonight, with its speeches and toasts, will be a kind of reunion for the former students. Many will bring their children and grandchildren. But the central figure of the events 60 years ago, Leonard Bates, will not be there.

He is listed as deceased in the university's alumni database. Mr. Spivey spoke with him in 1988, and it was very likely one of the last times Mr. Bates talked about his days at N.Y.U. He graduated from the school of education in 1943, then went on to serve in the military. He returned to New York and worked as a guidance counselor in the public school system.

Mr. Spivey told Mr. Bates that he was trying to track down the Bates Seven to interview them. Mr. Bates replied, "If whenever you do find them, tell them, 'Thank you.'"

Edward Wong

After the story of the Bates Seven ran, the following letter was received and published by The New York Times:

To the Sports Editor:

The impact of Edward Wong's article is being felt in ways that no one could have expected. The article has created a buzz far beyond N.Y.U. and informed untold people about the disgraceful practice of "sitting out" black athletes whenever opponents considered their participation offensive. This is to say nothing of the deserving attention it has given to these long-neglected individuals.

The article also made the historic, heartwarming, inspirational occasion at which the seven were honored even more remarkable than it already was. ABC, NBC and CBS local affiliates covered the event. *ABC Weekend News* closed its program on Saturday evening with the story. All did thoughtful and serious reports.

There is more, much more. Should anyone doubt the power of the pen, the following should make believers of us all. By all accounts, only six members of the Bates Seven were still surviving. The seventh member and only black, Argyle Stoute, was officially "unlocatable" or presumed dead because he was considerably older than the others.

Then, nearly one and one half hours after the tribute had begun, an elderly black man walked into the hall and all eyes turned toward him. It was Dr. Argyle Stoute, with a diploma from the Sorbonne in hand. He learned of the event from the article. Like Mark Twain, he came to prove that reports of his demise had been greatly exaggerated. Dr. Stoute, who has a psychoanalytic practice in New York City, knows a lot about head games. Once again, life imitates art.

I kept asking myself about the odds of six (one going through her eighth regimen of chemotherapy) surviving 60 years after their protest, let alone all seven. Prof. Aaron Tenenebein of N.Y.U.'s Stern School tells me that the odds of the six surviving minus Dr. Stoute is 317 to 1. Including Stoute, the odds increase to well over 11,000 to 1. As they did 60 years ago, the Bates Seven are still defying expectations and beating the odds.

Jeffrey T. Sammons

You've Got a Friend

HOUSTON, Tex.—Esther Kim and Kay Poe are best friends who live in Houston, Tex. They are both champions at the sport of tae kwon do, which is a lot like karate, except that tae kwon do uses kicking moves while karate relies more on the hands. Both of these young women had dreams of winning an Olympic medal in the 2000 Sydney games— which was the first Olympics where tae kwon do was included as a sport. And one day, a few months before those Olympics, Esther did an extraordinary thing to help make her friend Kay's dream come true.

To become a member of the American Olympic team, an athlete has to win a qualifying competition. Both Esther and Kay did well during their qualifying matches, until the semifinal round, when Kay hurt her knee so badly that she had to be carried down a flight of stairs on the back of her coach. Her next match—the final, championship match—would decide everything. The winner would go to the Olympics and the loser would stay home.

Kay's opponent in that match was her best friend, Esther. The two girls had trained together for 13 years. Esther loved Kay like a sister, and knew that her injured friend was in no condition to compete.

"We have to fight," Kay told Esther. "I'll do the best I can."

"You can't even stand up," Esther replied. "How are you going to fight?"

Esther knew how badly Kay wanted to go to the Olympics. Esther also believed that Kay deserved to go. But she knew that if the two girls fought, Kay would lose because her knee was injured. So Esther did something so amazing that, at first, the judges did not believe her. Esther forfeited the match—by refusing to fight, she gave the victory to Kay.

"I wouldn't be losing my dream," she thought to herself. "I'd be handing it to Kay."

"I really want to go to the Olympics," she then told her father, who is her tae kwon do coach, and who also coaches Kay. "But it's not fair to go out with two legs and her with one leg. I couldn't live with myself knowing I beat someone who had already been beaten."

Esther and her father helped Kay limp onto the mat. Both Esther and Kay were crying as the judges announced that Kay was the winner because Esther wanted her to be. "It felt like the only right thing to do," Esther said later that day. "It did hurt, but winning a gold medal isn't everything. There are other ways to be a champion. If I don't have a gold medal around my neck, it's in my heart."

Sometimes small moments come to mean something bigger than themselves. This was one of those moments. Esther's decision to help Kay caused many other athletes to take a new look at their sports, and to wonder what they would do if faced with the same choice.

"To make that sacrifice is an incredible gesture," says Jay Warwick, who runs the United States Tae Kwon Do Union, which makes the rules for this sport in the U.S. "Sport is so focused on winning and dollars and cents. When you see pure innocence demonstrated, it reminds you this is neat."

Esther's decision has also made people wonder whether she should have had to face such a decision at all. A country's Olympic team should be made of the best and most deserving athletes, these people say, not just those athletes who are having a good day during the qualifying match. If an athlete is hurt, but her record during the year is better than everyone else, shouldn't she automatically be on the team? Yes, says Donna Lopiano, who is in charge of the Women's Sports Foundation, a group set up to study these questions. "To force an injured player to play is unconscionable," she says, meaning that there is absolutely no excuse for it.

Esther says she did not plan to prove a point, and didn't expect to receive worldwide attention. "Kay has always pushed a little harder, always wanted it a little more," Esther says. Kay was also lucky enough to have a friend determined to help her.

Jere Longman

Both girls attended the Olympic Games in Sydney come September, Kay as a member of the U.S. team, and Esther as a guest of the International Olympic Committee. Esther was in the stands watching as Kay was defeated in an upset during the first round. "We are all proud of her," Esther said of her friend. "She hasn't let anyone down."

Riding a Bike Uphill

―――――――――――――――――――――――――――

Lance Armstrong is one of the best known names in the world of profes-
sional bicycle racing. Only one American racer was better known than
Armstrong when this story began. That was Greg LeMond, who was the
only American to win the prestigious and difficult Tour de France, a bike
race across France, that takes three weeks. It was thought that 25-year-old
Armstrong could do that one day, too. But he shocked and saddened the
world when he announced that the pain he had felt for months in his
groin—pain he had ignored—was caused by testicular cancer, which had
spread to his lungs, his abdomen and his brain. He began treatment with
chemotherapy and vowed to beat the disease and race once again. A few
weeks after Armstrong began his treatment, he was visited by reporter
Samuel Abt who wrote this story:

AUSTIN, Tex.—As mornings go, this one seemed ordinary: fog
masked the hills west of Austin, a light wind fluttered flags, the tem-

perature promised another shirt-sleeves day. About 7:30, rain began falling for half an hour and everybody said that was a good thing because there had been a bit of a drought in central Texas.

A commonplace morning for most people, but another wonderful, joyful morning for Lance Armstrong. He woke at 7 at his home on Lake Austin, went to the kitchen to prepare a pink grapefruit for breakfast, looked at the newspaper and then began celebrating another day of simply being alive. "Every day I wake up, I feel great," he said later. "I say, 'This is great,' because six months from now, a year from now, five years from now, I may not be able to say that."

"You can see where they did it," he said, lifting his blue Dallas Cowboys cap. He leaned forward to show the two stitched semicircles on the top left and the back of his head, where doctors removed the brain cancer. "I'm feeling fine," he said, "a little bit of fatigue, which means I have to take a nap every day, about two hours. This week I feel like I felt two months ago. I really do. That's no lie."

Armstrong will leave Monday for a week at the Indiana University Medical Center in Indianapolis, where he will receive four hours of chemotherapy daily for a week. It will be the third of four scheduled weeks of chemotherapy. The treatment will be administered through a tube that was fitted in his left chest and that he wears full time at home during the two weeks between each session. Taped over his heart, the outside of the device resembles the tube that bicycle riders use to pump air into flat tires. He has no interest in irony, though. He is concentrating on one thing only, and that is survival. That is why another morning alive is a triumph.

"It used to be when I woke up every morning, I knew I was going to wake up," he said. "It was so normal I took it for granted and now I never know. We're not promised anything. We're not promised tomorrow.

"We all expect to have long and fulfilling lives, but I suggest people not take that for granted. We don't always attack life, not do things to the fullest, and I suggest that people take advantage of life."

He was sitting in the living room of his new, white Mediterranean-style villa, which he helped design. This is the house he had dreamed about for years, perhaps even when he was a teenager living in Plano, outside Dallas, being raised by his mother after his father left when Armstrong was an infant.

"The home," he said, "I put a lot into it both in time and money and I really feel an attachment to this house because this was dirt before, this was level ground and we built it up, furnished it, did everything exactly the way I wanted it.

"When I started it, I must have been 22 and it showed that a 22-year-old can work hard, have success, financially do well and take on a big project like this and succeed.

"Now it means a lot less than it did before. Houses, cars, motorcycles, toys, money, fame—it takes on a whole new meaning when you have something like this. You realize, 'I never lived for that stuff.' I think something like this makes you not only look at your life but makes you simplify your life."

The tan that he has during the racing season has disappeared and he seems pale, understandably less buoyant than usual. He is holding his weight steady at 170 pounds, he said, although he admitted that some of his muscle has turned to fat despite daily bicycle rides of up to an hour and a half.

"I do feel good," he said. "I'm not as fit as I used to be, but then again for two months I haven't done much on the bike. I'm undergoing chemotherapy and I do have cancer, pulmonary lesions that are detrimental. But the lesions on the lungs are going away pretty rapidly.

"I'm really upbeat. I'm positive. I may be a little scared, I may be very scared, but I feel very positive about how things are going."

He said that measurements of the levels of proteins in his blood produced by the cancer have gone from a high point of above 100,000 to 113.

"Still a way to go," he said. "That encourages me even though the hardest part to knock out is the last part."

For now, he said, he is giving little thought to his career as a bicycle racer ranked ninth in the world. He has come a long way from the 19-year-old on the United States national amateur team who fended off questions about whether he was the next Greg LeMond by saying, "No, I'm the first Lance, the first Armstrong."

His goals back then were astronomic. "Win the Tour de France and you're a star; I'd like to be a star," he said then, half-jokingly. "I'm sure I'd get sick of all the pressure and all the appearances, but I'd like to try it." Now he has tried it for a while and, even though he has never come close to winning in four attempts at the Tour de France, he is a star.

Getting up from his chair to fetch another half grapefruit—"Citrus fruits," he said, "they definitely fight cancer"—he barely looked at a map of the next Tour de France that was lying nearby. "I think very little about that, maybe a quarter of the time," Armstrong said. "The other three quarters are focused on my life and beating cancer. If, for some reason, I can never race again, listen, that's fine."

The route of the Tour varies from year to year, and the next one will be mountainous, not always Armstrong's favorite terrain. It would be, he was told jokingly, a terrible Tour for him. "Cancer is a terrible Tour for me," he said. "The Tour de France, it doesn't matter. You know.

"I would love to race but nothing's going to make me happier than to live. Life is the No. 1 priority. Professional cycling is No. 2. No, to create awareness for testicular cancer is No. 2. Professional cycling is No. 3."

Did he feel it was unjust that he had cancer? "No, because cancer doesn't play like that," he said. "It doesn't play fair—nobody wants cancer. You can say, 'Why me?' But why not me? It doesn't strike because you've done something or not done something. I was just one of the ones it happened to hit. No, I don't want to waste my time saying, 'Why me?' I have a problem and I want to fix it."

Samuel Abt

Armstrong finished chemotherapy, and was declared free of cancer. That's good news, meaning that there were no more cancer cells in his body, though it was not a guarantee that those cells would not return.

After 18 month of treatment he started training again. Bicyclists race on teams, and Armstrong's team had cancelled his contract when he got sick. He could only find one team—sponsored by the United States Post Office—that would have him join them.

In his first race he finished 52nd among 70 riders. He married Kristin Richard, moved to France, and began to train for the Tour de France.

He did well from the start of the grueling three-week-long race. In fact he did so well that many could not believe that he wasn't cheating somehow. Samuel Abt wrote about the rumors:

ALPE D'HUEZ, France—Lance Armstrong has heard the rumors and doubts.

"Innuendo," the 27-year-old American calls speculation that he is leading the Tour de France because he is using illegal drugs. How else, some of the European news media are asking, can somebody who underwent chemotherapy for testicular cancer two and a half years ago be so dominant now in the world's toughest bicycle race?

The suspicion toward him is all the more intense because of a sportwide drug scandal that came to light in last year's Tour de France, and almost scuttled the race. Asked flatly whether he is or has been doping, Armstrong said, "Emphatically and absolutely not."

"I'm not stupid," he said as he had dinner at his team's hotel in the mountain resort of Alpe d'Huez. "I've been on my deathbed."

"My story is a success story in the world of cancer," said Armstrong, whose victory is by no means guaranteed with 10 of the 21 stages of the race still to go. "A lot of people relate to my story. In America, in France, in Europe, they relate to this story." The French fans, who know his story, respond with hearty cheers each time he is introduced at the starting sign-in and when, at the end of each stage, he dons another yellow jersey, the sign that he is still in the lead.

"And look," he continued, "I'm not going to get mad about the questions because I understand them after the events of last year. I expected this."

Few predicted before the event that Armstrong would lead the race by nearly eight minutes after winning 3 of the 11 daily stages so far: the short prologue, a long time trial, and then the first of two climbing stages in the Alps on Tuesday. He also finished a strong fifth in the ascent to Alpe d'Huez. He is climbing so powerfully now, a teammate, Kevin Livingston, said today that he could have won the stage to Alpe d'Huez but did not because he and the team did not want to appear greedy and make enemies among teams that circumstances might later cast as allies.

Speculation about the reasons for his performance mounted after his victory Tuesday in Sestriere, Italy. There were veiled references in newspapers and television to the power of a man who has never been known as a dominating climber and who did not return full time to racing until May 1998, more than a year and a half after his cancer was diagnosed and treated in the United States.

"There's no answer other than hard work," Armstrong said as he ate his way through two bowls of risotto topped with grated parmesan cheese, several slices of buttered bread and many glasses of mineral water. He finished with a slice of apple pie, which he decided was not all that good and switched to a slab of blueberry pie. "Much better," he judged.

Armstrong was willing, even eager, to discuss the rumors. Asked if he was taking any medication, he replied: "Vitamin C, multivitamins, those. This is the Tour de France, you need certain recovery products, but certainly nothing illegal."

Dr. Lawrence Einhorn, the oncologist who treated Armstrong at the Indiana University Medical Center, told the Associated Press that Armstrong is "98 percent home free" from the cancer. He said that Armstrong's treatment is completely finished, and that the rider is taking no medication for the cancer. As the race leader, Armstrong undergoes a urinalysis every day that looks for such drugs as steroids. Like everybody else in the Tour, he had a blood test at the start, which he and all other riders passed. These tests will be given occasionally, more or less at random.

The innuendo does bother him, Armstrong said, "for the sake of the sport. It's bad for the sport, so I can get worked up. It's disturbing for the sport. I think it's unfair."

He credited his climbing skills to a loss of weight, about 15 pounds to his present 158 pounds. Noting that he and his teammates spent weeks in May riding over Tour stages here in the Alps and in the forthcoming Pyrenees, he said, "This team has done more work than anybody else" in the race's pack of 20 teams.

The rumors of drug use proved to be little more than that. Armstrong finally said publicly that he had been using a steroid cream for a skin rash, and that racing authorities had approved its use. It was not strong enough, everyone agreed, to boost his performance. That he seemed to have done on his own. Determination, not drugs, gave Armstrong his power, though he acknowledged that he should have come clean about the steroid cream when questions first arose.

Samuel Abt was at the finish line when the Tour de France ended:

PARIS, France—Aglow in the yellow jersey of the champion, Lance Armstrong completed the final leg of his long journey to Paris today, winning the Tour de France 33 months after cancer threatened his life and appeared likely to end his cycling career.

Calling his victory a miracle, Armstrong, 27, became only the second American to win the Tour, the world's greatest bicycle race. He stood solemnly with his cap off as a French military band broke into "The Star-Spangled Banner" just after he was given one more yellow jersey, two more bouquets, a blue vase and a check for 2.2 million francs ($350,000).

A crowd of half a million people, watching under a blazing sun and pure sky, cheered him on the Champs-Elysees. "It's been a tough three weeks on the legs and head," he said after he crossed the finish line, well back in the pack, and just before he left the victory podium to embrace his wife, Kristin, whose face was running with tears. Then his team took the traditional victory lap up and down the Champs-Elysees, with Armstrong carrying the American flag.

"It is a miracle," he said. "Fifteen or 20 years ago, I wouldn't be alive, much less riding a bike or winning the Tour de France. I think it's a miracle."

Armstrong finished the 3,690-kilometer (2,290-mile) Tour a comfortable 7 minutes 37 seconds ahead of Alex Zulle, a Swiss with the Banesto team, and 10:26 ahead of Fernando Escartin, a Spaniard with Kelme. Of the 180 riders who set out on July 3, 141 remained today.

Armstrong described Greg LeMond, who became the first American to win the Tour in 1986 and won again in 1989 and 1990, as "a good friend of mine and the greatest American cyclist ever." But his victory and LeMond's were different, he continued, because LeMond rode for French teams and Armstrong "did it with an American sponsor and an American team, seven of the nine guys being Americans.

"That is, first of all, unheard of," Armstrong said. "Two years ago people would have thought you were crazy." Until this year, the United States Postal Service did not win a single stage of the Tour.

And for an encore? "There is nothing," he said. "If you win the Tour de France, the only thing you can do is try to win it again. That's it. Next year, I'll be here."

FAMILIES

SEPARATED AT BIRTH

GARDEN CITY, Long Island—As soon as Tamara Rabi arrived at Hofstra University, she noticed the bizarre behavior. People she had never laid eyes on would smile, wave and greet her as if they knew her. When Tamara stared back, blankly, they would walk away. A few friends claimed to have spotted someone who looked just like her. Someone else with long dark hair, she figured.

Then Justin Latorre, a friend of a friend, showed up at her 20th birthday party and could not stop staring. Tamara, he said, looked just like his friend Adriana Scott. As the other guests dug into ice cream cake, Justin asked Tamara questions. Like Adriana, he learned, Tamara was adopted. Both girls were born in Mexico. And they even had the same birthday.

Thus began the real-life fairy tale, the kind of story that inspires movies (*The Parent Trap*) and at least one sitcom (*Sister, Sister*).

Adriana, raised Roman Catholic in a house with a white picket fence in Valley Stream, on Long Island, and Tamara, raised Jewish in an apartment near the American Museum of Natural History on the Upper West Side of Manhattan, really *are* twins. Because of problems in the adoption process, they were separated at birth.

The twins' adoptive fathers both died of cancer, one of several similar things that have happened to them in their separate lives. Neither knew she had a twin sister, and Tamara's adoptive mother, also did not know. Adriana's adoptive mother knew, but did not know how to find her daughter's twin.

With Justin's help, Tamara and Adriana had their first contact— electronically—a few evenings after the birthday party. The two exchanged instant messages on their computers: Tamara was in her dorm room at Hofstra, with two friends by her side; Adriana was at home, with her mother. They learned that both were 5-foot-3¾, and that Tamara loves Chinese food, and Adriana doesn't.

Adriana's mother watched the instant messages fill the screen and she remembered how hard it had been to come back home from Mexico 20 years ago, bringing their new baby daughter with them but leaving her twin behind. They'd wanted to adopt both girls, but the rules of the Mexican adoption system made that impossible. Was this girl—Tamara from Hofstra—really that girl?

Adriana's mother knew only one thing about the other baby— that she had been adopted either by a rabbi or by a family named Rabi. So, as she stared at the computer screen, she told Adriana to ask Tamara's last name.

"Rabi," came the reply.

"When I saw it coming up on the Internet, that last name, I thought, 'Oh, my gosh, this is it,'" Adriana's mother said.

For Tamara, that same feeling came when Adriana sent a picture of herself by e-mail. Had it not been for the teeth straightened by braces and the absence of a birthmark near the right eyebrow, it could have been a snapshot of Tamara herself.

"The picture came up and our jaws dropped," said Christie Lothrop, 19, one of Tamara's suitemates who was standing next to her. "We didn't know what to do."

The twins agreed to meet the following Sunday in a McDonald's parking lot near Hofstra, a world away from the Guadalajara hospital where they had last been together. Tamara brought two friends; Adriana, who is a junior at nearby Adelphi University, brought one.

On the way, each twin panicked and suggested turning around. The friends would not have it. Identical twins separated at birth find each other on Long Island and then chicken out of their reunion? Forget about it.

Soon they were face to face, sisters who had grown up thinking they were each an only child. "I'm just standing there looking at her," Adriana recalled. "It was a shock. I saw me."

The group went somewhere else for lunch, where the twins sat side by side nibbling at chicken fajitas as their friends ogled at the similarities in their expressions, their gestures and how both rested for a few minutes mid meal, then resumed eating.

Later that day, at the Scotts' house, Tamara had trouble tearing her eyes away from the life she might have lead. There she was—well, Adriana, really, but it looked like her—captured on videotape, in a commercial for toilet paper. There she was, in a white frilly dress, for communion at the Church of the Blessed Sacrament. When Tamara finished a sentence with, "and, dah dah dah dah dah," Adriana's mother burst out laughing. It sounded so familiar.

Still giddy, the twins and their friends drove into Manhattan to meet Tamara's mother, who, because she'd never known her daughter had a twin, had her doubts about the entire story. Those doubts disappeared when her daughter walked in with a look-alike clutching childhood photos. "It was just incredible," Tamara's mother said. "You just blink your eyes and say, 'This can't be real.'"

The following weeks were a whirl of breathless e-mail, eye-popping surprises and constant retellings to anyone who would listen, which meant everyone. The twins paraded each other through their respective campuses, and to their part-time jobs. A Hofstra student interviewed Tamara for a class assignment, and a senior communications major asked to do his final project on the twins.

Tamara, who shares a name with a character on *Sister, Sister*, had for years been asked from time to time, "Hey, Tamara, where's your twin?" Now she had an answer.

But the twins and their mothers have also experienced other emotions, subtleties that those on the listening end of their story could not be expected to quite understand. What, after all, is the "right" reaction when you are an only child who suddenly has a twin sister with your voice, your olive skin and even a pair of silver hoop earrings similar to yours? And as a widowed mother, how do you feel watching your only child bond with a sibling?

From the start, Adriana said that finding a twin was a dream come true. In the weeks after their first meeting, she called Tamara often and invited her to parties, or announced that she was near Hofstra, and did Tamara want her to stop by. She placed a picture of both of them in a silver frame decorated with the word "sisters" that she had bought for a photograph of her sorority. She gave Tamara an identical frame. For Tamara, though, life was more complicated. Her adoptive father had just died, about three weeks before the big reunion. Finding Adriana was, at first, a joyous distraction. But the grief was still raw, and soon she felt overwhelmed.

Tamara did not always return her sister's calls, and she declined more invitations than she accepted. "It was hard to find out how to have a sister in your life when you've never had a sibling," she said. "We're not as close as people feel we should be."

Slowly, hesitantly, and sometimes still giddily, they are getting there, settling into their strange, unexpected sisterhood.

They have discovered that as children, they occasionally had the same haunting nightmare in which a loud sound fades into softness and then gets loud again, and that they both love dancing and started lessons when they were young.

When Adriana told Tamara about an audition for Entertainment Tonite, a D.J. company looking for dancers to help energize parties, they decided to go together. At the audition Wednesday night, the twins danced side by side, their ponytails swinging in sync as they learned the steps.

Elissa Gootman

In School with Their Children, Parents Try Again

CHICAGO, Ill.—As Larry Morris, a 39-year-old security guard and father of six, folded his six-foot frame into a desk made for 14-year-olds, his knees knocked against the desk rim and his back crouched stiffly in his seat next to a girl in a Bugs Bunny T-shirt.

It has been 22 years since he last sat in a classroom and carried a book bag. He dropped out of high school at 17 and in those 22 years, he had six sons and two wives, held minimum-wage jobs but was rejected for better-paying work because he had no diploma. He also grew up.

He decided he would never get anywhere unless he finished high school. "You feel less of a person," Mr. Morris said of life without a diploma. "You feel incomplete. You're reminded every day that you can't get anything but McDonald's. You have to go through that disgrace."

So now he is a high school sophomore again, taking notes in geometry or physical science, walking the same halls where he hung out as a teenager, attending the same school as his 17-year-old son Jermaine, but struggling two grades behind him. He goes to class before working eight hours as a night security guard.

Mr. Morris and six other older dropouts from long ago have returned to DuSable High School, the only school in the country with a program that allows parents to enroll with their children and get the diplomas they regretted not earning.

The parents are urban Rip Van Winkles picking up where they left off decades ago. "My first day was like when I went to kindergarten," said Ida Gardner, a 39-year-old junior and a mother of five. "I didn't know none of the kids."

As a condition of their enrollment, the parents must follow the rules like any other student. They are forbidden to smoke or leave the building during school hours, must show up at homeroom and eat mystery meat at lunch like the rest of their classmates.

The parents are easy to spot. They are the ones huffing and puffing up the stairs while teenagers bounce past them. They were like these teenagers 20 years ago, sneaking a smoke in the restroom, drumming pencils on desk tops and primping and flirting at their lockers before the bell. Now, that is all behind them. They are all business. They sit rapt, front and center, right in the teacher's face, copying down assignments as if their rent check depended on it, sometimes bored because they already did next month's homework.

"I bust my butt to be here," Mr. Morris said. "I don't have no time for no foolishness." The parents have been teased by some students who consider them intruders and some teachers who see them as failures. One teacher told a returning parent, "If you didn't get yours before, you should have stayed out there."

Many teachers wondered how they could teach with adults in the room. "We thought, 'Have they gone crazy?'" said Susan Wills, the work-study teacher. "'What has DuSable come to? Who are we to tell an adult anything?'"

The parents turned out to be model students. "When you ask for a report of a page, they do 10 pages," said Jim Westphal, an English teacher. "They can send me any parent."

The parents bring calm and wisdom to the building, and students are less likely to misbehave when the parents are around. "I don't want to be cursing and acting silly around them," said Alex Lee, a 17-year-old senior, eating pretzels in Mr. Morris's homeroom. "I got respect for old people. Some of them are 40, 45 years old. To me, that's old."

The parents try hard not to play teacher's pet. After all, they were hardly that the first time. But sometimes they can't help themselves. In his work-study class, Mr. Morris could not resist raising his hand when a student angrily complained that he's had to wait an hour for a job interview.

Mr. Morris told the student that those things happen sometimes and that people should not let it stop them from trying. Then, he started talking about the times he got the runaround looking for work, and another parent in the class shook her head in agreement.

"Here they go again," a couple of students said, elbowing each other.

Since then, the parents have learned not to say things like, "I have a son your age," or, "When I was a teenager."

The school has tried to prevent some teenage angst by not permitting parents and their children in the same classroom. But it still can put a cramp on a teenager's social life when his father's locker is down the hall. "My son wants to pass like two ships in the night and that's what we do," Mr. Morris said.

Walking to physical science, Jacqueline Fulton, a 39-year-old junior and mother of three, passed a lanky boy in a red T-shirt. "That's my nephew right there," she said, as the boy walked by without so much as a glance. "I just act like I don't know him either."

It is a measure of how uncool the whole proposition is for some teenagers that Mr. Morris's son is early for school nowadays. "He tries to beat me out the door," Mr. Morris said. "I would like to walk to school with him, but he gets out the gate first. When I try to catch him, he's gone."

In the case of Mrs. Gardner and her son, Kwante, it is she who hates to run into him in the halls, fearing it is only a reminder that she did not finish school.

"I duck and dodge; I don't want him to see me," Mrs. Gardner said. "He says, 'Hi Mom,' and I keep walking."

When the parents first arrived, some students made fun of them, pointing and demanding an explanation. They asked, "What are you doing here?" or, "Aren't you a little old to be in school?" In one class, Mr. Morris had to stand up and spell out who he was and why he was there.

"It's as if the kids were saying: 'This is our domain. Can't we have anything to ourselves?'" said Mrs. Wills, the work-study teacher.

At times the resentment has turned ugly. The other day, Ms. Fulton, who never learned to read well before and is now struggling to learn, stumbled over some words when reading aloud in class.

"She must can't read," shouted a boy in the back.

"That's the reason I'm here," Ms. Fulton said. "If you was any type of person, you wouldn't sit and criticize me. You would help me."

The tears welled in her eyes. Mr. Morris, sitting beside her, put his arm around her and said: "It's going to be all right. You know you got to expect that here."

The parents' presence has made for some unexpected scenes. The principal, Charles Mingo, recalled the day he saw what he thought was a girl beating a boy in the hall. "I thought to myself, 'Oh no, I got a fight on my hands,'" Mr. Mingo said. "I looked closer, and it turned out it was a parent and her son. He should have been in gym class. She popped him right there in the hall and marched him off to the gym."

More than anything, teachers say, the parents are living proof that dropping out is not glamorous. Like reformed smokers, they will step in when they see students making the same mistakes they did. When a parent saw a classmate sneaking out of class to be with her boyfriend, the parent told her: "You don't need to do that. I did that. That's why I'm still here. If you know like I know, you'll stay in school."

The current class passed its first milestone last week when report cards came out. All the parents did far better than they did the first time around, except one mother who Mr. Goodman said was "reliving her childhood again" and got all F's for poor attendance.

On report card pickup day, Ms. Fulton had her 58-year-old mother, who has difficulty walking, come to school to sign for her grades as if she were 16 again. The teachers told her mother she was making progress and "gets along well with the kids."

Beaming, Ms. Fulton showed her report card to anyone who would look. "I never been so proud in my life," Ms. Fulton said of her A, two B's, two C's and D. "I got to frame this."

Isabel Wilkerson

A Family Home at Last

SCRANTON, Penn.—Married 12 years, in love for 22, Barbara and Charlie Smith have created 17 children. When strangers find out this fact, they don't know how to react.

"Some people have that look, you know, and they ask 'Oh my God, how do you do it?'" Mrs. Smith said as her youngest, 18-month-old Steven, lolled underfoot and the eldest, 18-year-old Chad, took a break from painting a bedroom of his own, the first he has ever had.

Mr. Smith, who delights in the size of his family, rolled up his left sleeve to show his tattooed list of the children's names.

"Here they are, every one of my little kiddies, except . . ." He paused and squinted about, checking the tattoo against the impish faces scattered around him.

"Except the three youngest," Mrs. Smith said. Then everyone

laughed at her husband's struggle to recall all the names and everyone joked that, well, he always has another arm.

Dad's difficulty was not hard to understand. Keeping the names straight was complicated by the children's fondness for nicknames. So let the record show that the children, in order of eldest to youngest, ran somewhat as follows:

Chad, Brian (Bri), twins Ashley (Betsy) and Eric (Feedhead), Danielle (Megan), Dustin (Bundy), Charles (Chewy), Kricket, Casey (Pie), Bristy (Starla), twins Trysta (Gaga) and Kysta (Kooter), Kaylee, Skyler (Howie), Shawn (Mikey or Bighead), Corry and Steven (Puggy).

For much of the past year the family was not living together, because they could not find a big enough house that they could afford. The home they had lived in for years was condemned by the city, and the Smiths were evicted. Each morning Mr. and Mrs. Smith had to travel all around town, collecting their children from all the friends who had given them a place to sleep, then taking them to school. In the evenings they would gather everyone together again, so the family could have dinner together, after which they would return to separate houses.

"We were together and the next day we were all scattered," Mrs. Smith, 43, said of the bad spell when even the city's welfare and housing agencies despaired of finding them a place that was big enough and affordable.

"The kids were afraid we'd never be back together again as a family," she said. Finally the city agencies gave up and asked the American Red Cross to help them, as a disaster case.

"Who's going to take in a family of 17 kids?" asked Robert E. Quinn, the director of Habitat for Humanity for Lackawanna County. "These days the government can't handle it when you have 17 kids." But because of Mr. Quinn, the family does have a home. And the Smiths are so grateful, they have given him a nickname of his own. "Hey, Ozzie, what's happening?" a pug-faced tyke (Chewy? Bighead?) shouted from the porch of the Smith's 10-bedroom home given to them by Habitat for Humanity. The house itself is 80 years old, and hundreds of volunteers worked to fix it up so the family could live there. Habitat requires that the new owners help with the work as a way of "earning" the house, and the Smiths have in more than 2000 hours of hammering, sawing, plastering and painting.

"Lifesavers," Mr. Smith said of Habitat and the Scranton residents who rebuilt the house and donated 16 roomfuls of furniture. "You don't see a large family today; especially you don't see a large family that's still together."

Across the dining room, his wife tended some of the children and said gently, "No more problems. I don't consider the kids a problem."

Mr. Smith, who has made his living by helping children get on and off school buses, said he was eager to take on the $150 he would pay to own the home. The fright of seeing his family homeless and fractured had made him desperate, he said.

"We were at the point of pitching a big tent," he said as he looked about his home. "If it wasn't for my kids, I'd have gone off the deep end. I look at the act of God and he comes out and says, 'Bite your tongue, hold your peace, and you'll make it through.' And that's what we've been doing." There should be a "victory celebration," not a mere housewarming, Mr. Smith said.

Francis X. Clines

WHEN HUBERT, 85, MET MILDRED, 73

NEW YORK, N.Y.—Love stories—they're a dime a dozen. The soaps are full of them, and they overwhelm the pages of novels and the movies. The plots are built of the same basic ingredients. Who needs another love story?

But it's constantly young love, occasionally middle-aged love. Who will sing of nursing home love, wheelchair love, love on the borders of life's end?

So, if you will, one more love story, in time for Valentine's Day.

The Sarah Neuman Center is a nursing home in Mamaroneck, N.Y., part of the Jewish Home and Hospital network. Its 300 beds are occupied by the old and the frail, people mostly winding down their lives, thinking more about yesterday than tomorrow. One of them is Hubert Spurr, 85. It could rightly be said that love brought Mr. Spurr into the nursing home and then abandoned him there.

His wife arrived first. Her name was Lucy, but everyone called her by her childhood nickname, Bubbles. She was his second wife, and they had been married for more than 20 years. Their love was an enviable love, an incandescent love. And then Alzheimer's chose her. For years, Mr. Spurr cared for her at their Westchester home, until it was no longer possible, and she moved into the nursing home.

Most of his life, Mr. Spurr worked as a telegrapher, retiring at 64 from United Press International. Then he fished and he traveled a lot with his wife. He was not robust—he had injured himself during a bad fall on the street and was wobbly—but was able to continue to live in his own home with some help. Yet he couldn't bear the thought of separation. Soon after his wife's arrival, he moved into her room, and continued to care for her with unstoppable devotion. It was who he was.

This was their life, until last year, when Mrs. Spurr, at 92, died in Mr. Spurr's arms. His own will died with her. There was nothing more he wanted out of life, not a thing. He missed her so much that he cried every day.

"I want to die," he would say to others in the home. "I have no interest in living."

Sorrow proliferates in a nursing home, amid the surge and ebb of enervating lives, but the rhythms of the home continue. Meals, medications, physical therapy, movies, bingo.

Five times a week, a sullen Mr. Spurr reported to physical therapy. Sometimes, the patients are taken down early, creating a traffic jam of wheelchairs waiting their turns. One morning, a month after his wife's death, Mr. Spurr was there early. He found himself positioned beside a woman named Mildred Bobe. She was 73, a youngster in a home where the average age is 88.

When he gazed at her, he could see she was as consumed with grief as he was. And he could see something else: black eyes that hypnotized him. Oh did he adore those eyes.

Until her health betrayed her, she had enjoyed a contented life. She worked as a supervisor in the data entry department at Salomon Brothers and lived with her three cats—Ivory, Ebony and Max—in Flushing, Queens. She had known love, but never marriage. Life unfolds that way for some people, and she was untroubled about the outcome. She had had a couple of proposals from men who were appealing in many ways. But what stopped her was her sense that they had wayward eyes that would never remain fastened on her.

"Nice fellows," she would say. "But I always saw the flaws."

She continued to date often enough, for she loved to dance, but she was satisfied with the single life. Her relatives knew her as Spinster Millie.

Then her health deteriorated—she had several heart attacks—and she left her job in 1986, and slowed down. She joined the local Kiwanis Club and became its president. She fraternized with neighbors. It kept her busy and happy.

Her health worsened. She had a weak heart, diabetes, high blood pressure, a malfunctioning kidney. She had help come in. One day, she found herself on the floor and unable to get up. Her older sister in White Plains tried to care for her, but it was too much. Ms. Bobe reluctantly entered Sarah Neuman.

She hated being away from her home. Here she was confronted with all the dreaded afflictions of old age: disability, dependency, loneliness. Her days seemed to be more about dying than living. When she went to occupational therapy, she would have a hood or towel draped over her head and she often fell asleep. She couldn't muster the strength to brush her teeth.

At that first encounter, as they waited their turns, Mr. Spurr began talking to her. He encouraged her to really work on her rehabilitation; it would make a difference in her life. He used to hunt and fish, and he regaled her with stories on those subjects. Ms. Bobe found his descriptions engrossing. She liked this man. "And he's a handsome-looking man," she said.

She perked up. "He told me I have beautiful eyes," she said. "I fell for that. Even after all these years, I fell for that."

They began spending time together, talking during their therapy sessions, doing activities together. They both like history. One day, they had a good discussion about Rasputin.

He found himself renewed. "I wanted to live again," he said. He began to understand that old age was still about hope.

But a change of plans was afoot. Her sister, Rochelle Rospigliosi, was moving to Seattle with her husband and wanted to take Ms. Bobe along to live with them in their new home. A month after they met, Ms. Bobe shared this news with Mr. Spurr.

Distraught, he tried to talk her out of it. It wouldn't work; how could she be sure she would get the right medications, have her meals made just the way they had to be made? It seemed all too risky. She couldn't go.

And of course there was another factor: what would he do without her? Something was going on inside him. He would never have thought it possible. His 85-year-old heart was in love again.

Feelings were stirring in her as well, yet the prospect of being back out in the world was a potent lure. She planned to go to Seattle.

One day Mr. Spurr suggested they visit the nursing home's gift shop. By now, he had bought her various gifts there—a necklace, a watch, a bracelet. While she browsed, he whispered to the proprietor, "Give me the most expensive ring you've got."

The woman pulled it out. He liked its look, the best in the shop, $18. He slipped it on Ms. Bobe's finger.

"I don't want you to go to Seattle," he told her. "Stay here and marry me."

At once, she said, "Yes."

Marry after knowing each other a few weeks? Wasn't that sudden? She: "Not at 73. The future is now."

He: "I figured at 85 I better take whatever opportunities presented themselves."

Both of them came to the nursing home expecting to wait out the end of their lives. Neither suspected they would discover a new beginning.

When she heard the surprise development, Ms. Rospigliosi had an are-you-kidding reaction. "I prayed a lot," she said. She went to the nursing home to meet Mr. Spurr, and then she eased up on the prayers: "We all just fell in love with Hubie."

To improve on the $18 ring, Mr. Spurr had his daughter get a nicer engagement ring for Ms. Bobe.

The nursing home has been abuzz with the news. The engage-

ment has lit up the entire place. The porters call Mr. Spurr Loverboy
or The Man. Not surprisingly, there is some jealousy. One woman
who has been cordial with Mr. Spurr huffed to others, "I saw him
first." She's 92.

Feb. 13 was chosen as the wedding date, the day before Valentine's Day. The home's rabbi will preside over a civil ceremony in the
winter garden, followed by a reception that the home will cater. All
the residents are invited. The couple could have registered at the
nursing home's gift shop, but has decided against gifts. "Where would
we put them?" Mr. Spurr said. "We don't have the room."

Ms. Bobe's niece, Barbara Pomer, will be the maid of honor, but
most of the rest of the wedding cast is being assembled from the staff
of the nursing home. One of the therapeutic recreation leaders will
be best man. The ring bearer will be the son of a worker in the
finance department. The piano player will be a woman from the
therapy department. Another therapeutic recreation leader is doing
the floral arrangements (he was once in the flower business). A
maintenance man will sing "Spanish Eyes." One thing is particularly
important to Ms. Bobe. This is her first wedding, and she certainly
intends it to be her last, and she wants to walk down the aisle. So
does Mr. Spurr. Both use wheelchairs, and for a while, they considered doing it without walkers, but they realized they don't want to
risk falling and spoiling the mood. So they plan to use walkers, but
not wheelchairs. It has to look good.

Mr. Spurr had been living with a roommate in Room 310 and Ms.
Bobe and her roommate are in Room 202. Once they are married,
they naturally want their own room. Right now there is no vacancy,
and the home can't predict when they can be accommodated. Only
death opens up rooms. A couple of weeks ago, though, when there
was a death on the second floor, the home moved Mr. Spurr into the
space. Now, at least, he is only a few doors away from his heartthrob.

Through the halls of the nursing home, they wheel, their faces
alive with joy. They are rarely apart. He gets behind her in his wheelchair and pushes hers.

They go to bingo together, where the prize is a 25-cent voucher.
He refuses to go on Saturdays, because the prize is merely candy, and

so she skips those games too. They attend a cooking class. They watch TV in his room, though she leaves at 8:30, because her roommate goes to bed early and she doesn't want to disturb her. They like to go to the communal TV room for the 4:30 "Sherry Hour."

"You get like an eyedropper full," he said.

"It's better than nothing," she said.

They await the big day. Soon it will happen. Then they will be what they most want to be, husband and wife, now and forever.

N. R. Kleinfield

Getting by with a Little Help from His Friends

BANGOR, Maine—It was a year ago when Zach Woodward, a junior at Bangor High School, asked his mom if Brian Raymond could move in with them. Once again, Brian had no place to live. Brian Raymond and Zach Woodward had been best buddies since third grade and stayed close, even when it became clear that something was terribly wrong at Brian's house; even when Zach, a popular boy, was ribbed by other friends for hanging out with Brian. "What do you always have to bring Brian for?" they'd ask.

"Mutt and Jeff" is what Zach's father called them. Zach is 5 foot 4 inches and 130 pounds; Brian, 6 foot 4 inches and 230 pounds. As to why they're friends, Zach says, "He's so big, he protects me," though it isn't true. Of the two, Zach is the athlete, a tennis and hockey player built like a concrete plug. Brian is more a gentle giant, a bit of a computer geek.

"For a while people felt I was addicted to my computer," Brian says. Zach's mother thinks the reason they're so close is that ever since they were little they were two boys who loved books.

Sophomore year, when Brian's mother entered the local mental hospital, he began living on his own in apartments, with friends, in a room at someone's house. To pay his way, Brian worked after school at Service Merchandise, a department store, and started a computer repair business. His guidance counselor, Jim McNamara, would ask if he was eating; Brian would assure him that he was, though there were many nights when there was no food in the apartment.

Brian is not a boy to complain, so it took a while for Mr. McNamara to figure out how hard his life was. Looking now at Brian's transcript, he can see that 10th grade was the low point. Brian had always been a math and science whiz. "He got a C in Algebra II," Mr. McNamara says. "That should never have been."

When Zach asked his mother about Brian's moving in, Bridget Woodward said, "I have to talk with your dad"—Mark Woodward, the editor of *The Bangor Daily News*—even though she knew it would fall mainly on her. Mrs. Woodward, an aide in the local office of Senator Susan Collins, is finicky about her home, and kept mentioning the extra laundry, the food and how they would fit everyone's beverages in one refrigerator. But what she was thinking was, "Do I want all this responsibility?"

Zach was hopeful: "Mom didn't say no. She said she had to think about it." The truth was, Mrs. Woodward liked Brian. She was impressed that a boy with so hard a life had such nice manners. She remembered how on summer mornings when he was little, before all the Woodwards were awake, he was at the house calling for Zach. She told him not to come by until 10, and after that, you could set the clock by it: summer mornings at 10, Brian at the door.

In the end, Mrs. Woodward said yes. And if she had not? "I don't know," Brian says. "Kind of what I've been doing is going along and hoping it works out. I never had too many options."

It is hard to know why life's weight sinks some children while others, like Brian Raymond, keep bobbing up. Part of Brian's good fortune is that good people have helped at the worst moments: the Woodwards; Mr. McNamara; his girlfriend's family, the Irelands, who took him in for short stays, made sure he had food and clothes and gifts on his birthday; Gerry Palmer, a businessman who helped Brian start his computer repair service; and Irv Krupke, a teacher who let him use the computers in drafting class whenever Brian had a free period.

But there is more to it. People seemed willing to do so much in part because Brian rarely asked. "He's very soft spoken, doesn't push himself on somebody," Mr. McNamara says. "People respond." While Bangor is a small, blue-collar city of 34,000, few here know Brian's story. When a reporter arrived from New York to spend a day at the high school, a secretary said, "Which Brian Raymond do you want?" (Turns out that there's a freshman Brian Raymond, too.)

Brian knew how to blend in. "If you look at Brian," Mr. McNamara says, "you don't see a kid who seems to come from the depths of poverty. He keeps himself clean, dresses well, knows how to get along with people and what he needs."

His advance-placement computer teacher, Stephanie Lord, says the only hint she had that something was amiss was when she sent home progress reports to be signed by parents and Brian's came back with a waiver from the principal.

Which is not to say he's perfect. "He is a teenaged boy," Ms. Lord says. He drinks Diet Pepsi at 8 A.M., talks too much in class with Brian Webber (Deanna Jones, the English teacher, is constantly yelling, "Brians!") and can be lazy if the subject doesn't appeal to him. "I don't think he's even read the last two books," Mrs. Jones says.

He hasn't. "I like reading," he says, "it's just the 'Epic of Gilgamesh' and stuff like that doesn't really interest me." While most top students took an S.A.T. prep course, Brian did not. "I didn't want to spend the money," he says. "I figured that I would do well enough."

He did: of a possible 800 he scored 690 in math and 730 on the verbal.

His mother was a factory worker, his father managed a truck stop, and though the father also suffers from a mental illness called manic depression, Brian says, "No one saw it for a while."

By sixth grade, it was plain. In a manic phase, he says, his father spent all the rent money; in a depressed phase, he sat in the living-room chair all day. "Since he tried to commit suicide, he was not the same," Brian says. "The whole family had to go to counseling. My counselor said my defense mechanism was to separate myself from the rest of the family."

Brian spent hours alone in his room. "I had my computer. That was it."

After his parents divorced, his mother had a breakdown and was also hospitalized.

According to school records: "The quality of his family life deteriorated drastically. . . . His mother, who was living with a male friend rather than at home, would call to check up on Brian and his sister. They received . . . inadequate financial support from her. There were days without food . . . Brian's sister . . . and many of her friends would come to the house to party and spend the night. . . . This situation became intolerable for Brian."

His one joy during sophomore year was Erika Ireland. They met in middle school, where they both were in gifted classes, but as Brian says: "I didn't pay much attention to her. She was real quiet. I talk a lot." In 10th grade, they had the same English class. This time when Brian talked, Erika talked back. "One day," he says, "Erika said she'd seen me walking home from school and I ought to stop by her house some time." He did, that day.

"I was walking down the hill by my house," Erika says, "and he came up behind me singing loudly." It was Brian's way of saying hello. That night, Erika's mom insisted on driving him home. Brian had her drop him in front of the Woodwards'. It took the Irelands months to piece together the truth. "I didn't want to scare them off," Brian says now. "They have a normal situation."

In his junior year, Brian's guidance counselor told him that he could get a legal-aid lawyer and become emancipated from his family. "Brian went there by himself," Mr. McNamara says. "He was that determined." On Jan. 23, 1997, Brian's petition for emancipation was granted.

These days, Brian's biggest problem is senioritis. He can't wait to get out of high school and on to college. And while he's still known as a computer guy—he wrote the program Mr. Krupke uses for all his drafting classes—he's known for other stuff too, like being Erika's boyfriend.

Brian has been accepted to several engineering programs, including the one at the University of Maine in Orono and the Rochester Institute of Technology in New York. Erika will go to Orono and thinks Brian should, too. "It makes a lot more sense than Rochester," she says. "Rochester's a 12-hour drive. Half the people he fixes computers for are in Orono—it'll be a strong base for his business."

Brian is not sure. He has been all over cyberspace but never in an airplane and is tempted by a faraway place. "Every day Erika and I fight about it," he says. "I don't know."

Even Mrs. Woodward admits that Brian has fit in nicely at their home. They converted a small study for his room and bought a second refrigerator, so there is plenty of space for everyone's beverages. It is the most home Brian has known. "Those places I rented," he says, "I just had a fridge and had to stay in the room. Here, I can sit down, watch TV. It's more like I live here; it's kind of cool."

Mornings at the Woodwards are hectic. Mr. Woodward's rushing off to the newspaper, Mrs. Woodward to the Federal building. The boys are always late and eat their pancakes standing at the kitchen counter. One pancake is plenty for Zach; Brian eats four.

Mr. Woodward once asked his wife why she bothered cooking pancakes every morning instead of letting them grab cereal. His wife told him those boys would remember those pancakes the rest of their lives.

Michael Winerip

LANGUAGE

APOSTROPHES

BOSTON, England—Apostophes jump out everywhere at John Richards, and he sees the little squiggles of punctuation as a sign of the declining standards of our time. Just four blocks from his house, for instance, is the Print Xpress copy shop, with its sign offering to print "menu's." (Correct English, of course, would read *menus*.)

Everywhere you look, Mr. Richards says, apostrophes are running amuck. Taking a reporter on a grammatical tour of his neighborhood he stopped at the sign in front of "the modern mans barber shop." (It should be *man's*.) There was a store featuring "ladies fashions" (which should read *lady's*) and a pub whose weekly current events board was titled, shockingly, "whats on." (*What's* would be correct.)

"It's irritated me for years and years," says Mr. Richards, who is 75 and has retired from his job as a copy editor, where he corrected grammar, punctuation and spelling. He doesn't understand why people insist on forgetting to put apostrophes where they should be and inserting them where they should not.

A few weeks ago he decided to act on his annoyance. He formed the Apostrophe Protection Society (the only other founding member was his son, Stephen). Then he drew up a form letter and began delivering it to offending businesses in the area.

"Dear Sir or Madam," the letter begins. "Because there seems to be some doubt about the use of the apostrophe, we are taking the liberty of drawing your attention to an incorrect use."

After explaining the punctuation rules, the letter concludes, "We would like to emphasize that we do not intend any criticism, but are just reminding you of correct usage should you wish to put right the mistake."

The campaign has had limited success so far, with only one establishment actually correcting anything. (That was the local library, which changed its "CD's" sign to "CDs.") In general, Boston business owners do not share Mr. Richards's passion for punctuation.

"Sounds to me like this man wants a job," Reginald Dunmore, a local butcher whose van advertising "carvery's" earned him a letter from Mr. Richards.

But if Mr. Richards is a man with an obsession, it is an obsession many Britons share. The Telegraph, a British newspaper, ran an article about the Apostrophe Protection Society, and within a day Mr. Richards had received 50 letters from well-wishers, many of whom joined the group on the spot. The issue is an emotional one, judging from the writers' accounts of their own apostrophe-related battles. "Some of them are quite a bit more militant than I am," Mr. Richards said. "One person said he carries round sticky bits of tape with apostrophes on them, and sticks them on as required."

One woman wrote movingly about her outrage when a pub in her area displayed signs for "todays menue's" (today's menus) and "Nigels special pudding's" (Nigel's special puddings). "I tried to correct the notices but was restrained by my husband," she related.

In another case, a letter writer described her fruitless battle with the local branch of Sainsburys, a supermarket chain that removed the possessive apostrophe in its name (*Sainsbury's*) but put it in the wrong place in the parking lot, where the sign reads "shopper's car park" (*shoppers'* would be correct, because there are usually many customers in a store at one time and the lot is for all of them).

"I suggested they were perhaps being too modest in only expecting one shopper to turn up," the woman recalled. "They didn't even reply."

Mr. Richards has the straight posture of a man used to standing up for himself. He is all too aware that his fight against the greengrocers' apostrophe, as it is known because of the tendency of fruit-and-vegetable stores to advertise "apple's" and "orange's" (in place of *apples* and *oranges*), is not universally popular. Even some experts seem unbothered by this casual use of apostrophes in nonpossessive plural situations.

"Greengrocers might do it out of ignorance, but it is also being used intentionally to draw attention to what you are selling," Jean Aitchison, the Rupert Murdoch professor of language and communication at Oxford University, told *The Telegraph*. "In the informal setting you can do what you like. That's the way language works."

But for everyone willing to bend the rules of punctuation, there is also someone like Ian Senior, an economic consultant who seethes daily at the fact that his village is called Kings Langley, having long ago dropped an apostrophe from King's (unlike Boston's neighbor King's Lynn).

For years he has been fighting to bring the apostrophe back, and he even brought the subject to a vote at an annual town meeting. But though the villagers voted in favor of apostrophe restoration, 80 to 8, they were overruled by the council.

"They initially said they would have to change all the stationery," Mr. Senior said in an interview. "I said, 'Let the current lot run out and print new paper,' and then they said, 'What about the road signs?' There was no appetite for making a change."

As for Mr. Richards, the correspondence spurred by his apostrophe campaign has reminded him that there is a big, imprecise world out there, with many outstanding grammar and punctuation problems.

"The incorrect use of 'fewer' and 'less' is another thing that annoys me," he said, warming to that subject but checking himself just in time. "If I carry on, I'll get quite worked up."

Sarah Lyall

An Old Language Lives

OKAVANGO DELTA, Botswana—In the beginning, there were the rushing rivers, the whispering reeds, the "Kwa! Kwa!" of shrieking herons and the rumble of lions. When the Wayeyi people drifted here some 200 years ago, they thought they had found paradise.

They settled in huts along the green marshes and built canoes to glide through the twisting streams. They fished, harvested water lilies and named the animals, flowers and stars in their language—Shiyeyi.

"First, first people to come here are Wayeyi and Bushmen," said Baagi Letsapa, as he guided his canoe through the sleepy waterways.

He is a leathery man who still remembers the teachings of his father. He knows that the boiled roots of the sage plant help ease indigestion, that papyrus makes the best sleeping mats and that the ukayi plant produces a poison that kills fish, but not people. This knowledge is disappearing as young people abandon the rivers, the canoes and the old ways. But not without a fight.

Here in the swamps of northern Botswana, the Wayeyi are battling not to disappear. They are just a tiny group in a country dominated by the Tswana people, and for generations tribes like theirs
have been discouraged from practicing the traditions that make
them different from each other so that there is only one national
way. But a few years ago the Wayeyi decided their traditions were too
important to fade away. They took the government to court and
demanded that their tribe be officially recognized and that their all
but forgotten language—a language only the elders of the tribe still
speak—be taught in schools.

Critics said they were asking for trouble and that they would pit
one tribe against another. Young people are not interested in the old
ways, the critics also said. All across southern Africa, young people
have left small villages and moved to the cities. Urban teenagers
groove to the hip-hop singer Wyclef Jean, teeter on platform heels
and gleefully meld English and African languages into a boisterous
slang that rattles some grandparents. A new generation rolls its eyes
at village traditions.

But to the critics surprise, the high court handed the Wayeyi a
startling victory. The court struck down the law that recognized
the existence of only Tswana tribes in Botswana. It ruled that the
law unfairly discriminated against the Wayeyi and was therefore
unconstitutional.

As word of the judge's decision spread, the elders started celebrating. Some dared to dream that the Wayeyi might someday see
their very first representative take a seat in the nation's House of
Chiefs, which serves as an advisory board to the government.

Others started to believe, for the first time, that they might actually save their vanishing traditions and language. "It's not just about
our chief; it's about our identity," said Lydia Nyati-Ramahobo, dean
of education at the University of Botswana, who helped prepare the
paperwork for the lawsuit against the government.

"Our language was dying," said Ms. Nyati-Ramahobo, who is also
the coordinator of the Kamanakao Association, which promotes the
language and customs of the Wayeyi. "The culture was dying."

Now there is hope that it can be saved.

In the nearby town of Maun, an annual festival celebrates traditional dancing and music. There is a Shiyeyi calendar and a Shiyeyi-English phrase book that includes a smattering of history for tourists and for young people who have forgotten their roots.

The book reminds readers that the bright star that signals the start of the fishing season is traditionally praised as "nyena mayiwa," mother of the sun. Elephants are known as "wadjovo." Leopards are called "wangwe." To offer friends and relatives good luck, the Wayeyi traditionally blew into each other's ears.

This week, the caretakers of culture gathered under a tall tree to share their stories. They were old men with silver hair and fraying shoes. Some had crooked legs and trembling hands. Others had straight backs and powerful voices. All had hope in their eyes.

The elders described the discrimination they had encountered from more established tribes. They described being dismissed as a backward people, feeling ashamed of their origins.

"We had no voice," explained Jacob Moeti, a 64-year-old traditional leader. "We were not a people who could stand up and speak and expect anyone to listen. We were looked down on. Even now, people are afraid to say they are Wayeyi.

"But we have now stood up and the courts have now heard us," he said. "We hope the equality will now make us equal as a people."

The old men grinned and some cheered. Someone chimed in, "The struggle is not over!"

But in many ways, the gathering of old men only made it clear how much has been lost. The village elders all conversed in Setswana, the language of the dominant Tswana. None spoke more than a word or two in Shiyeyi.

These days, only a few men still use the traditional skills that were passed from generation to generation in their everyday lives. Mr. Letsapa is one of them. When he was a boy, his father taught him how to navigate a canoe. Today, he ferries tourists through the swamps.

Mr. Letsapa says he is proud of the new push to preserve the old ways. But as he drifted through the swamp, he confessed that he was doubtful that young people could be lured back to their traditions.

"My son stays in town," Mr. Letsapa said. "He doesn't want to come here. In town, they don't know canoes. They know the car only. Me, I like to speak Shiyeyi; it's my language," he said. "But the young people now, they don't want to use Shiyeyi. And I don't know if that will ever change."

Rachel L. Swarns

Brazilian English

RIO DE JANEIRO, Brazil—If Aldo Rebelo gets his way, it will soon be illegal for Brazilians to go to a "drive-in" for a "hot dog" and "milkshake," entrust their cars to "valet parking" or invest their money with a "personal banker."

The activities themselves will not be prohibited, mind you, just the use of the English-language terms by which they are commonly known here.

Mr. Rebelo, a member of Congress, thinks there is too much English in Brazil, where the official language is Portuguese. He looked around one day and noticed stores everywhere with English names: The Pet From Ipanema; World Top Lock; Fashion Mall; Bad Kid; Video Market; and Sweet Way.

And he worried that Brazilians who don't happen to speak English would not be comfortable shopping in their own stores. "Why should Brazilians have to feel embarrassed in their own country because they can't pronounce these names?" Mr. Rebelo said.

So he is introducing laws which would outlaw the use of foreign words in this nation of 170 million people. This would "boost the self-esteem of the people in relation to Portuguese," he said, "and show them that it is not a language that is ugly, underdeveloped, backward or useless, as some people might imagine."

Mr. Rebelo said he was particularly alarmed by the use of English-language terms in business and technology when "there are perfectly adequate Portuguese-language substitutes."

Brazil has the largest computer and Internet industry in Latin America, and English-derived verbs like startar, printar, attachar or deletear and the nouns homepage, e-mail, site and mouse are standard usage.

Not everyone thinks that Mr. Rebelo's idea is a good one. "I think he and the whole idea are nuts," said Ricardo Gouveia Botelho, a 28-year-old Web site designer shopping at a computer store. "We use those words because everybody in the world understands them. And what does he plan to do, send the language police to the office to bust us?"

Although the bill was at first treated as a joke by some in the government, it was approved during a vote in the lower house of Congress—probably because they thought this debate would distract people from the real problems facing Brazil, like a growing political corruption scandal.

Since then, some business have begun reacting as though they expect this bill to become law. Major banks have ended programs with names like Hot Money, Federal Card and Home Banking, while stores have begun taking down signs that advertise a "sale" or "20 percent off" and replacing them with others announcing a "liquidação."

But most language professionals maintain that the legislation is too extreme and that it forgets the fact that English has not really taken over Brazil; instead, Brazilians have adapted English to their own needs. In fact, English words become so different when they reach Brazil that native English speakers often can't understand them. To Brazilians a shower stall is a "box," a billboard is an "outdoors," to go jogging is to "cooper" (after a doctor who introduced it here) and a razor blade is a "gilete."

Language experts warn that passing this law would mean eliminating much of the vocabulary of soccer, the national sport, since so many of the words there have roots in English. Here the game is called futebol, and includes such terms as gol and pênalti. But Mr. Rebelo said he was willing to grant an exception for words that had already become part of the Portuguese language.

Future violations, however, are another story. Those violators, Mr. Rebelo says, should be fined, or sent "back to school for Portuguese classes."

One reason Brazilians like Mr. Rebelo are worried about their language is that Brazil is the only Portuguese-speaking country in the Western Hemisphere. Because the country is surrounded by the Spanish-speaking nations of South America, the government has made Spanish a required subject in Brazilian schools, and some here are worried that their language will disappear entirely.

Larry Rohter

FRENCH ENGLISH

ROISSY, France—There is calm once again inside the control towers here at Charles de Gaulle airport just outside Paris. Air France's decision to do what was once unthinkable—make its pilots speak English to the control towers—lasted a mere 15 days.

The airline had the idea that safety considerations were more important than pride in language. Instead of having pilots talk to the towers in two languages—which can confuse pilots from other countries—the goal was to have everyone speak English, as happens at many European airports already.

But it wasn't so easy. Last month, the airline was forced to admit that it had underestimated both how hard such a change would be and how proud and stubborn French pilots and air controllers are about their language.

There was so much arguing over the subject during work hours that everyone agreed that the distractions were making it less safe to fly, not safer. So the plan was abandoned—at least for now.

France has long fought to preserve the purity of its language. There are at least 15 separate government committees here looking to create French words to match terms—usually English—that threaten to creep into the French language. For example, there were no French terms for "computer chip," "hacker" and "startups." Instead of accepting the English versions, the government went ahead and made new French words up.

Knowing this, Air France did not try to switch all its flights and towers to English at one time. It had planned to go slowly, only asking its pilots to speak English here at Roissy, near Paris. But some complained that since they spoke English outside of the country, French through the rest of France and then English only as they approached this airport, they were getting confused.

"For the first few days, the controllers said, 'O.K., it's a little difficult but getting better,'" said Jean Jezequel, the manager of air traffic control at the airport. "But then we began getting comments that it wasn't working at all. It was bringing tension into the control room and the controllers were saying that sometimes they just didn't know what language to use."

Suzanne Daley

FARAWAY PLACES

Moscow Traffic Jam

MOSCOW, Russia—There is a very big, wide, busy road that forms a ring around Moscow. It's official name is Moskovskaya Koltsevaya Avtomobilnaya Doroga (meaning the Moscow Ring Automobile Road), but everyone calls it by its acronym, MKAD, pronounced "muh-COD."

At 7 P.M. one December evening, 23-year-old Andrei Bogdanov got on the MKAD, intent on spending a snowy evening with friends who live near an interchange some 20 miles away. Unfortunately, there was a traffic jam. He did not reach his exit until 11 A.M. the next day. The most amazing part of this story is that this 16-hour traffic jam did not even make the news here. Traffic in Moscow can be that bad.

To be fair, this particular day was not a good time to be on the MKAD. A four-inch snowfall had made driving tricky. That morning, thousands of people swamped the newly opened Ikea furniture store south of town, overloading the ring road. And as every good Russian knows, Friday is the day to leave work early and head to one's country cabin, meaning main roads are already clogged.

But this did not deter Mr. Bogdanov. That evening he left his job at a downtown Moscow computer firm and set out for his friend's neighborhood. He pointed his 1998 silver Subaru station wagon east until he reached the MKAD interchange, where he entered, heading north.

Rather, he tried to head north.

"I was driving on the outer side of the ring road. All the roads toward the city center were blocked by cars—they were jammed," he said. "Gradually, I drove up to Yaroslavsky Road, where we actually stopped completely."

It was now 9 P.M. He dialed his wife on his cellular phone to say he was stuck in a traffic jam. Over the next two and a half hours, his Subaru moved about 45 yards, which is like not moving anywhere at all.

About midnight, Mr. Bogdanov saw strange doings among drivers in another lane. Getting out of their cars and waving their arms about, they were trying to organize all the cars in the area—hundreds of them—to move backwards at the exact same time. It didn't work. The bumper-to-bumper traffic inched along. Mr. Bogdanov passed a few exits, but he couldn't leave, because there was not enough room amid the traffic to change lanes.

By 1 A.M., drivers began abandoning their cars.

At about 2 A.M., visitors began appearing on the other side of the road—the side that was moving well, in the opposite direction. These were relatives of the stranded drivers who had been called by their stuck relatives from their cell phones and had arrived bringing warm clothing, food and gasoline.

It was now 2:30 A.M. Entrepreneurs who smelled money to be made began to walk between the jammed cars with bags of home-made sandwiches, hawking them to starving drivers and passengers.

It was 3 A.M. Everyone, it seemed, needed to go to the bathroom. But the MKAD is fenced in by tall, soundproofing walls, leaving no private place to seek relief. So four drivers edged their cars into a bumper-to-bumper rectangle, creating a kind of a Porta Potti.

Despite the occasional headlight and 5-degree cold, it was extremely popular.

It was 4 A.M. Tempers long held in check began to flare. A band of furious drivers ordered a truck driver to turn off his idling engine. He refused. They shattered his window. Meanwhile, radio stations made no mention of the jam.

At 6:30 A.M. Mr. Bogdanov managed to edge off the ring onto an obscure side road. He immediately became hopelessly lost. He edged southward until he again found the ring road where it looked like the traffic had begun to move. So he took his chances and got back on the MKAD, only to discover that the moving cars he had seen were merely other lost drivers like himself.

It was 7 A.M. The sun rose.

It would take another four hours and, in all, 10 gallons of gas for Mr. Bogdanov to complete the 20-mile trek to his friends' house.

Asked today about the huge traffic jam, a senior inspector at the department for propaganda of the Moscow traffic police said, in essence, that it never happened.

"The situation became stable in two or three hours," said the official, who refused to be identified. "All the drivers had a chance to leave the ring road. There were many exits. There is no way they could just stand there for 16 hours."

The official conceded that a man died during the tie-up. "He died from heart insufficiency," the official said. "That could happen to anyone."

Just the same, Moscow newspapers report, the traffic police have issued a bit of holiday advice for Moscow motorists. From Dec. 20 to Jan. 10, the advisory said, it is probably better not to drive at all.

Michael Wines

Advertising for a Wife

WOBULENZI, Uganda—Ahamadah Ntale has a vision for a new way for men and women to relate to one another here in Uganda—starting with him. A few weeks ago, he walked into the local office of one of Uganda's national newspapers and left the reporter with a story that ran with this headline: "Man hunts old woman to marry."

He is 25, a scooter taxi driver. He said he wanted a woman between 35 and 45, loving and free of AIDS. Most important, she would have to reverse Uganda's long tradition of men paying the family of a bride for the right to marry her. Instead, the article said, the bride-to-be must cough it up to *his* parents.

The first call came at 7 A.M. the day the article was published, from a 38-year-old businesswoman in the capital, Kampala. By nightfall, there were 193 phone calls, he said, and in the next week more than 400. One woman promised 10 cows if he chose her and gave up the search.

The question is, why are women so interested in this obscure taxi driver from a small town? One answer is: because they can be.

In the last decade, women in Uganda have made major progress toward equality—much more so than in other African nations. Women now know how to read, and the capital city of Kampala is full of working women, chatting on mobile phones and making money. The vice president of Uganda is a woman, as are several other leading politicians.

Now Mr. Ntale would like to give Ugandan women another right that only men traditionally have—the right to pay someone to marry them. "I want to see if women could support me, as men have always supported women after we have married them," he added. "I want to experience the way they treat us after marrying us."

Mr. Ntale is the second child of his father's third wife. His father, a Muslim, has 5 wives and 23 children. Every so often when Mr. Ntale was growing up, one of his sisters would disappear with a strange man.

"So I said to my mother one time: 'Why do they take my sisters?'" he said. "She said to me, 'They take them to get married and when they marry the men have to pay something.'"

"I asked one time, 'Why don't they take us, the men?'" he said. "She replied to me, 'The men pay for the women, not the women for the men.'"

That did not make sense to him when he was a child and it does not make sense to him now, he says. So when he decided it was time for him to marry he went to see a newspaper reporter to find himself a bride who will reverse the tradition.

"In the beginning I thought that he was joking," said the reporter, who clearly knows a good story. "But he stayed here for over two hours. He proved to me that he was serious."

The story ran eight days later, with the mobile phone number of one of Mr. Ntale's neighbors. The first call came when Mr. Ntale was still asleep, and the calls, logged by name in a book, have not stopped. The youngest caller was 27 years old, the oldest 60. (They actually had lunch together but he disqualified her because she is possibly a relative.) Several women have driven here, about 30 miles north of Kampala, one in a Land Rover and another in a nice Toyota.

Apart from the cows, he will not discuss what he has been offered by the women who want to marry him. He says that he wants his bride to have money, but that he will not necessarily choose the one with the most.

"I am not after some rich woman," he said. "I've seen a lot of rich women but they were not my choice. She needs to love me very much."

In his small town, he said, he has been congratulated by men and women alike. Dozens of men have begged him to send any extra women willing to pay dowries their way.

Ian Fisher

THE DENTIST ON THE CORNER

LAHORE, Pakistan—Mohammad Aslam uses pliers, wire cutters and a metal file on the mouths of patients he treats in a dusty, smelly public park.

Mohammad Ishaq Khan, who, like Mr. Aslam, calls himself a dentist, believes that toothaches have nothing to do with teeth. "If there is something wrong with someone's teeth, I can instantly know there is something wrong with the digestive system," he explained.

And Muhammed Jameel has never gone to school and cannot read or write. "I learned it in Karachi from a Chinese guy," he said of his job as a dentist. "I was 10 years old when I started."

The three men are among thousands of street dentists who provide crude "dental care" to tens of thousands, possibly hundreds of thousands, of pitiable patients a year in the avenues, parks, buses and trains of Pakistan. Like all astute retailers, they congregate where there is a large amount of foot traffic. Excruciating to watch in action, they chop cavities off live teeth, insert metal wire into the center of dead ones and use metal files to shave down false teeth that have been inserted into patients' mouths.

"I indulge them in conversation and when they are distracted I use this," Mr. Khan said, hoisting a metal probe with a razor edge. "Pain only goes away with pain."

The legions of street dentists here are a testament to Pakistanis' high pain thresholds and desperate poverty. Nearly a third of Pakistan's 140 million people live below the international poverty line, and earn less than $37 a month. Having a false tooth inserted by a licensed dentist can cost $40.

"I can't afford it," explained Mohammad Sajjad, a factory worker who recently asked Mr. Jameel to repair a front tooth damaged in a fight two and a half years ago. The pain, he explained, had started to bother him.

As Mr. Sajjad sat on a small stool on a pedestrian footbridge over a set of railway tracks, Mr. Jameel pried out brown chunks of dead tooth and flicked them onto the red plastic tarp spread out under the stool. At one point, the amateur dentist lit up a cigarette to smoke as he worked. At another point, a locomotive passed under the bridge, belching black diesel smoke onto the instruments and into the patient's mouth.

The factory worker showed no sign of discomfort as Mr. Jameel filed down his false tooth. He did not even complain when his gums started bleeding. Throughout the ordeal, he winced just twice. Afterward, he admired his new tooth in a small hand-held mirror and thanked his dentist.

"I came here a year ago for work on another tooth," he said. "It's good quality."

Pakistani health officials say they have tried to force the dentists off the street, but the demand for their services is too great.

"It happens across the subcontinent," said Dr. M. Rashid Anjum, assistant secretary of the Pakistan Medical and Dental Council, a regulatory group. "It's the poorest people usually."

Hygiene also appeared to be spotty. Mr. Jameel worked with bare hands. When blood from the factory worker's gums ran onto his hands, he just wiped it off with a cloth. He and other street dentists said they constantly clean their instruments—in a form of locally distilled moonshine.

Novel medical theories abound. Mr. Khan, the dentist who said that toothaches are caused by digestive problems, went on to say that brushing your teeth is harmful because it damages your gums. The smooth-talking 54-year-old said it is better to use your finger and an herbal medicine he sells.

"The medicine we give has such a sweet fragrance that they can go to any party and they won't have bad breath," he said, thrusting a pungent concoction that smelled like nail polish and peppermint under a visitor's nose. "You just need two drops."

Mr. Khan, who has a ninth-grade education, has been practicing dentistry in the park across the street from Lahore's main railway station for 38 years. He is also a tattoo artist. A boisterous man with a neatly trimmed white beard, he suggested at one point that a Western medical education could not match his secret treatment for whitening teeth.

"A person who's got a degree from America or Britain can't do it," he said, referring to his method of removing brown stains from teeth. "But I can."

But he and a half dozen others interviewed also appeared to have some sense of their limits. All said they never pull teeth, preferring to leave that to real doctors.

All had at least a partial set of dentists' tools and used the same type of enamel false teeth as licensed dentists. They said they buy their tools, teeth and glue from dental supply stores.

Mr. Aslam, one of the "dentists" who worked in the park in Lahore, said outsiders and wealthy doctors may laugh at their work— "the foreigners find it amusing"—but they are helping impoverished people.

Dr. Anjum, the regulatory official, said he wished that Pakistan had the luxury of eliminating street dentists. But for now they provide dental care that, if crude, would otherwise be unavailable.

"If there is a person who can relieve your pain, who can provide some sort of medical treatment," he said, "you may feel obliged to him."

David Rohde

COINS IN THE FOUNTAIN

ROME, Italy—The Trevi Fountain has stood in the center of this city for more than 200 years, and for almost as long visitors have thrown coins into its waters, hoping their wishes would come true.

But what has happened to all the coins that have landed in the fountain? It seems a lot of them have gone into the pockets of Roberto Cercelletta.

Every day, in the dark of the night, he would empty the treasure from the fountain, scooping up the coins with a rake or a magnet. The work took about 15 minutes, and he often raked in about $1,000. The police paid little attention for many years until an Italian newspaper wrote about him. One morning soon after, when he took his usual pre-dawn wade, police officers were watching, and arrested him. His black sneakers were still soggy more than three hours later as he waited in a nearby police station to be hauled off to jail.

"I wasn't really collecting all that much," said Mr. Cercelletta, a homeless and mentally ill man. He also said that he was sharing the money with other needy and troubled people; that someone else would be looting the Trevi if he were not; and that the arrest ignored more than three decades of tradition.

"I have no right," he said, "but I have been doing this for 34 years."

The officers who listened or wandered by during the interview had to smile. "He's historic," one said, explaining that Mr. Cercelletta's exploits had been well known to them for many years. In fact, officers have never really known what to make of him, or what to do with him. For a long time, it was not clear that he was breaking any laws.

The coins thrown into the fountain were not really anyone's property, so Mr. Cercelletta was not guilty of theft. But the coins were traditionally sent to Italian charities, meaning that Mr. Cercelletta deprived them of tens of thousands of dollars every year.

The only law Mr. Cercelletta was actually breaking was not passed until 1999. That was when it became illegal to wade into public fountains like the Trevi. So for several years the police had been periodically fining Mr. Cercelletta for entering the fountain, but not for taking the coins. He ignored those fines, and they could not prosecute him because he was homeless and they usually couldn't find him. Also, he did not seem to be keeping much of the money, so he had no money with which to pay his fines.

The police say they did not try very hard to prosecute him, because, for a long time, no one realized how much money he was taking. Mr. Cercelletta, on the other hand, said he knew the fountain was a money maker the moment he first saw it 30 years ago, and over time he has had to chase others from his territory.

He also had to create a system. The coins under the water are from dozens of different countries, so he had to take them to the bank to be converted into Italian coins that he could use. And his life became much more complicated when all of Europe switched to the Euro. Until then, he said, most coins stuck easily to his magnet, but the Euro did not so he had to wade into the fountain to scoop them up, thereby breaking the law more often.

Tourists who visited the fountain on the day of his arrest expressed a range of feelings when they learned where their coins may have ended up in the past. Delores Burgos, a native of New York who is now living in the Middle East, said that what Mr. Cercelletta was doing was "pretty smart, but kind of mean." Her children had made wishes, she said, adding, "He would have been stealing my kids' wishes." Her husband, Jeff Burgos, took a softer line. "It was only like 27 cents," Mr. Burgos said.

Frank Bruni

Several days later, Frank Bruni wrote another story about the fountain, describing how word of Mr. Cercelletta had given many other people the same idea:

An enterprising angler of sorts who illicitly fished the Trevi Fountain for a small fortune in submerged coins may have done more than attract the attention of law enforcement officials here.

It is also possible that he started a trend.

Rome police officials said they caught a 41-year-old Italian woman today as she waded into the 18th-century fountain and scooped up nearly $200 in coins that tourists, following a time-honored tradition, had thrown into it.

"We are extremely worried that this media coverage could have, as an effect, the phenomenon of copycats," said Massimo Improta, a senior police official. "So far, this woman is the first case. We are also hoping that it is the last."

BEIJING BRICKS

BEIJING, China—If you were to prowl the back streets of central Beijing any evening, you might find a spry gray-haired man, dressed in sagging undershirt, shorts and sandals, rummaging through demolition sites.

Working in the hot-pink glow of smog-charged sunsets, Feng Baohua mumbles with renewed pleasure every time he makes a find. He is digging for stones that once formed Beijing's ancient city wall. It was a wall that stood for hundreds of years, but then, during the 1950's and 60's, it was torn down and the bricks were used to build factories, houses, toilets and pigsties.

"Look, this one has a character written on it!" Mr. Feng said to no one in particular, gazing at the etched date that can still be seen on many of the 400-year-old blocks.

The old bricks are heavy—weighing about 44 pounds apiece. Mr. Feng chiseled modern cement off two of the blocks and heaved them onto the back of his rattletrap bicycle. Then he hauled his precious cargo to a construction site about a mile southeast of the Forbidden City, where the government is rebuilding a short stretch of the old wall.

Several years ago, officials started appealing to the public to return any original bricks they held or knew about, and citizens have brought in somewhere between 120,000 and 400,000 of them, depending on which official you ask. But that is still a fraction of the number needed just to form the outside layer of a remade wall, a construction manager said.

So Mr. Feng, a 55-year-old worker in a local chemical plant, has made these bricks his mission. There is a lot of construction going on around Beijing, and old buildings are being toppled to make way for new ones. As those old houses and factories are torn down, Mr. Feng is racing, with nothing more than his chisel and a bicycle, to rescue as many of the antique bricks as possible before they are carted away.

"I'm just an ordinary citizen, and I don't know much about grand ideas," he said as he examined the fresh debris of a house.

"But I wonder, how are we going to help the next generation imagine what our city wall was like?" he said, recalling how he enjoyed climbing on the structure as a boy.

The wall he remembers stood until after the Communist victory here in 1949. Mao Tse Tung, the leader of Communist China, thought the wall got in the way of his plan for a city filled with industrial smokestacks So in the 1950's and 60's, virtually all of the wall was torn down as the city built a subway line underneath and a highway along much of its path.

Today only a few of the ancient towers remain. The names of the old gates—Peace, Facing the Sun, Victory—have survived chiefly as highway exits on the city's Second Ring Road.

Somehow, though, large fragments of the wall remained standing along a southeastern section. Even people who lived in that neighborhood did not know the sections of the wall were there, because they were hidden by other buildings. Now these remaining pieces are being pieced into a larger wall that will combine new and old bricks.

But the public quickly became bored of searching for old stones, and Mr. Feng is one of the only people in town who are still looking. His loyalty to the project has made him a legend among the workmen who are actually building the new wall.

"Old Feng is very persistent," said Xu Ziwang, the on-site manager from the city's Relics and Ancient Building Construction Company. "He comes here three times every night, bringing in six more bricks."

Others in town can't believe that Mr. Feng is doing all this work for no pay. Modern bricks are worth something, they say, and can be sold back to construction companies for a few pennies a pound. But the ancient bricks are worthless.

One night while Mr. Feng was scavenging, a smartly dressed woman rode up on a bicycle. She was the former owner of the demolished house and she was surprised to find a stranger digging in the ruins.

"What are you doing with my bricks?" she called out.

She relaxed when neighbors assured her that the man was only taking worthless old ones for donation.

"If they aren't worth anything, I don't care if he takes them," she said with a shrug. "It's really got nothing to do with me."

Erik Eckholm

PESO PINCHERS

BUENOS AIRES, Argentina—Only a few years ago, no respectable wealthy Argentine would have dared show up in public carrying a shopping bag marked "Coto." That's because Coto is a low-cost supermarket chain and for a long time it was used only by people who didn't have a lot of money. But now it has become a store for everybody.

Women wearing black leather pants, fur coats, leopard-skin prints and scarves tied neatly to their necks are standing on the checkout line at the Coto store on the outskirts of the fashionable La Recoleta district. The economy is doing badly here, for rich as well as poor, so everyone is looking for a bargain. The rich are still snobby here, and they still care about name brands and status, but there is a new way to be fashionable now. In the words of a recent headline in *Clarín*, Argentina's best-selling newspaper, "To be austere is now in style."

The trend is sweeping, and it goes up and down the economic ladder of South America's wealthiest country. Less wine, more soft drinks; soap instead of shampoo or shaving cream. Fewer theater visits, longer lines for free cultural events in parks. All but the wealthiest are flocking to discount outlets and convenience stores.

Going-out-of-business signs are becoming more common every week, even around La Recoleta, while Coto booms in a neighborhood more traditionally known for Ralph Lauren and Louis Vuitton.

"We used to buy fun, unnecessary things that we liked," said Alicia Bóveda, a 54-year-old housewife looking over cocktail glasses at Coto. "Now I touch, I look, and I don't buy." She said she now buys strictly what she needs, and comes to Coto looking for bargains.

"There used to be a certain prejudice against us," Alfredo Cicala, 45, Coto's store manager in La Recoleta, said with a smile. "But we are penetrating a class that used to resist us."

Mr. Cicala said his store was succeeding because more people wanted bargain cosmetics, kitchenware and clothes and were shunning expensive specialty stores. He noted a booming business in motor oil and home tools as more consumers do their own repairs. In the last year, Coto has introduced its own line of televisions and stereo equipment to compete against costlier name brands.

Every shopper at Coto seemed to have a different reason to save. Mariá del Carmen Ingelmo, 62, retired a few weeks ago as a criminal judge. "My husband, who is a lawyer, and I make a good living," she said while looking at lower-priced wines at Coto, "but some of my husband's oldest clients are simply not paying him on time. We used to change cars every two years—for each of us—but now, just forget it."

Josefina Santamaría, a 19-year-old university biology student in a blue-jeans jacket, said dating had gotten more expensive in these hard times. "There are still guys who are willing to pay—at least on the first few dates. Then, its fifty-fifty because money is tight." She added: "I used to go to the nearest store and buy without looking at a price tag. Now, I compare supermarket prices carefully."

If these changes last it will mean that Argentina is becoming more like the United States, where even rich people like a good bargain.

Clifford Krauss

Monkey Man

DELHI, India—Rumors spread like viruses in this city, where the streets are narrow and a shortage of electricity means the lights are often out. For more than a week, a rumor swirled that a creature—half man, half monkey—was being spotted around the city, and every night crowds of excited young men brandished tridents, bamboo poles and iron rods, ready to battle something that probably doesn't exist.

Those who have seen it—or who think they have—describe it as either a slinky cat with tawny eyes, a bounding black bear, or a masked superhero. But most often it is described as half monkey, half man. People who claim to have spied it say it leaps effortlessly across rooftops, scratches with long, poisoned metal claws and vanishes into thin air.

"I saw it with my own eyes," exclaimed Harish Singh, 16, who pulled out a gleaming foot-and-a-half sword he had tucked into his pants for protection. "When the ladies started shouting on the ground floor, we went to the roof. We saw a small black creature hiding in a corner, and suddenly it just disappeared."

As he spoke, a group gathered around him, and people began to tell of their own sightings. Deepak Sharma, 18, declared in tones usually reserved for ghost stories, "It was a strange kind of black shadow, a strange kind of animal no one has ever seen before."

The police patrolled night after night, looking for the creature, but found nothing. That is because there is no such animal, they say, just wild imaginations and bad dreams caused by India's hot summer air. But to calm everyone down and show they are trying, the police have also offered a reward of 50,000 rupees (a little more than $1,000) for information leading to the apprehension of "the mischief monger."

Manoj Lall, deputy police commissioner in East Delhi, said the rumors had traveled across the country, stopping in one city after another, until they reached this capital. It was believed mostly by poor and uneducated people whose knowledge comes from rumor rather than newspapers and books. "It is fear of the unknown," he said. "It has taken the shape of myth."

The Indian Rationalist Association, which believes in fact and science, has called the rumors "mass delusion." Sounding a lot like Sherlock Holmes, the group noted that the creature has left no footprints.

The only good news is that burglaries have simply stopped because so many people are not sleeping, and are standing guard at their homes, the police say. "Even if a dry leaf crackles, they think that a monkey has arrived," said Rajiv Ranjan, a Delhi police official who has been chasing down some of the hundreds of monkey-man calls that have poured into station houses over the last week.

Even rumors, though, can hurt people. A pregnant woman tumbled down the stairs of her home in Delhi as she fled in terror because she thought she'd heard the monkey-man; a man fell from his roof as he tried to escape the monkey-man. Both died. In a third case, a man dreamt that the creature was pulling on his sheet; he cried out and frightened a neighbor who then leapt from the rooftop in fear.

To calm the fears, government officials have stopped cutting electricity at night, so that people did not have to walk the streets in the dark. That only helped a little. "We want the government to take care of this," said Krishan Kumar, an embroidery worker. "We want safety."

But how do you keep people safe from a story?

Celia W. Dugger

CLOSER TO HOME

Enforcing the Law

John Tierney, a columnist for the Times, wanted to see whether dog own-ers could be persuaded to keep their dogs on leashes—in keeping with the law—while playing in New York City parks. Here's what happened:

NEW YORK, N.Y.—I started at 8:30 one morning in Riverside Park. Three-quarters of the dogs on the promenade were running free, and their owners, as usual, were ignoring the law that said dogs had to be leashed between 9 P.M. and 9 A.M. But I didn't confront the owners who were breaking the law. Instead, I went up to an el-derly woman with two dogs on a leash, introduced myself as a reporter, and gave her a $20 bill along with a certificate.

The certificate was called a "Big City Civility Award," and it pro-claimed: "You are hereby awarded the sum of twenty dollars ($20) for engaging in civil behavior in a public place. Thank you for keep-ing your dog leashed. Please accept this small prize from our organization, Big City Civility, as a token of your neighbors' gratitude for making New York City a better place to live."

The woman looked at me suspiciously. She grabbed the certificate without looking at it but refused the cash. "Nyet, nyet," she said, in Russian, waving it off as she hurried away.

A young woman nearby also with a leashed dog did agree to accept the $20, but she, too, looked leery. And once I explained the purpose of my crusade, she handed me back the money.

"I don't deserve it," she said. "I had my dog off the leash back there before you saw me." She agreed to accept a $5 civility award along with a new certificate saluting her for telling the truth, but she was still not happy.

"I feel awkward," she said. "Why are you giving money away? I'd rather just be thanked." If nothing else, the experiment had already confirmed the theory that New Yorkers will complain about anything, even free cash.

A few other dog owners were similarly wary, but most had no trouble pocketing the cash. One woman held up the bill to her golden retriever and announced, "Dog biscuits!" A man with an Australian shepherd took the money and urged me on.

"I completely agree with the goal of your group," he said. "It's a problem for joggers and old people because the dogs will run up to them. People with small children worry that the dogs will run them over. I worry that an aggressive dog will come up and attack my dog." He doubted, though, that any amount of money would entice the offenders to leash their dogs. "They're absolutely militant about letting their dogs run free. The only thing that would stop them would be more patrols and stiffer fines." Other owners seconded that opinion.

Some dog owners yelled at me. "That's very noble of you to give out awards," said one woman whose dog was running free. "But you are obviously not a dog owner. Would you put your child on a leash for $20? That's how we feel about these animals." She and the other dog owners argued that it was a fair compromise to let dogs run free in the early morning hours when the park was mostly empty.

I persisted for three mornings over the course of the next week, handing out a total of $240 to the small number of owners whose dogs were leashed. As I hoped, the news of the awards spread quickly among the other dog owners along the promenade.

But the money didn't really change anyone's behavior for long. A week after the experiment began, the percentage of unleashed dogs at 8:30 A.M. was just as high as before.

John Tierney

An Officer and a Gentleman?
50 Women Would Disagree

ALL OVER THE COUNTRY, United States—He proposed to Karen. He proposed to Yana. He proposed to Monica. He proposed to Kathy. He proposed to Sarah. He proposed to Susan. He proposed to Vicki. He proposed to Colette.

You get the idea.

Col. Kassem Saleh of the United States Army was part of the force that fought the Taliban in Afghanistan, a task fraught with peril and often lonely. But apparently not that lonely.

The Army said yesterday that it was looking into allegations that he managed to line up dozens of prospective wives in the United States and Canada, women he met through Internet dating services. Virtually all of them posted advertisements on a Web site which specializes in men and women who are taller than average.

In recent days, as his chronic courting has come to light, some of the women have compiled a list of more than 50 women who were romanced by him. The women are heartbroken and intent on revenge. They have complained to the Army that they want to see him punished and even thrown in jail. It's unclear at this point if his behavior, if proven true, violates either criminal law or Army regulations. Col. Roger King, a spokesman for the Army's 18th Airborne Corps at Fort Bragg, N.C., where Colonel Saleh is now stationed, confirmed that the Army was investigating the matter and that Colonel Saleh had no comment on the allegations.

According to Colonel King, Colonel Saleh is a 29-year Army veteran who headed reconstruction and humanitarian efforts for the American-led military operation in Afghanistan until his tour ended last month.

Through his efforts, the duped women maintain, he managed to attract someone from states all around the country, including Alaska and Hawaii, and two from Canada. They range in age from 33 to 57. One encountered him years ago, others just a few months back. A few actually met him in person, some of the women said.

It's not that the colonel, who is 50 (though he gave various ages to the women) needs a wife. He is already married, the women said.

The matter began to unravel after a television station in Washington, KNDU-TV, showed a segment in April about a woman in Pasco, Washington, who was engaged to Colonel Saleh and awaiting his return from overseas. That story was posted on the MSNBC Web site. Soon, other women who thought they were Colonel Saleh's fiancée called KNDU. According to these women, Colonel Saleh was a two-timer of massive proportions. They now derisively refer to him as "Kassanova."

Robin Solod, 43, lives in Manhattan and is studying to become a real estate broker. For four years, she said, she had worked the Internet dating scene, looking for a man who would tell her he would be by to pick her up on his motorcycle. Instead, she found men who owned bird collections or played golf. Last November, she placed an ad on a tall personals site (she is six feet tall) and Colonel Saleh answered. "He responded with a beautifully romantic e-mail," she said. "He said I was beautiful, I sounded wonderful. He wanted to get to know me."

She said he told her he was fighting in Afghanistan. A week later, he called her by satellite phone, saying that he was in a safe house in Afghanistan. "He sounded like Don Johnson," she said. He wrote her daily e-mail messages and made phone calls to her that sounded dangerously exciting:

"Baby, I love you . . . vehicle coming!"

"What proceeded were the most intoxicating love letters," she said. "He wrote better than Yeats. He wrote better than Shakespeare. He totally intoxicated you with his feelings: 'Oh, baby, I want to tell you how much I miss you. I can't wait to get home to you.' "

In one e-mail message that she provided, he wrote: "You are my world, my life, my love and my universe. It's like my mother used to say to me in Arabic when I was a little boy. Yi yunni (my eyes), Ya hyyetti (my love), Ya elbee (my heart) and Ya umree (my life). She used to sing it to me so I would fall asleep in our one-bedroom apartment in the slums of Brooklyn."

In fact, one of the other women said he mainly recycled letters he got from one woman and sent them on to the others. Or he would cut and paste letters he received from different women and create new ones that went out in bulk.

Ms. Solod said he told her he had been divorced 10 years ago and had not had a relationship since. He was waiting for the one perfect woman.

"There was this connection I felt," Ms. Solod said. "Unfortunately, there were 50 of us who felt it." Two months ago, she said, he called her and proposed. She said he told her: "You're the most significant woman I've met. You're just like my mother."

Even though she had never seen him, she immediately agreed to marry him. "Crazy, right?" she said, recalling the moment.

She read the MSNBC dispatch at the end of April. "I almost had a heart attack," she said. "I e-mailed him within one second. He e-mailed me back within one second. He said, 'Don't be silly, she's only a friend.' "

She managed to track down the woman in Washington and

found out the truth. Since then, many of the women have been com-municating with one another. One woman e-mailed some of the others, saying she tried to commit suicide last week. "We're all trying to support her," Ms. Solod said.

Sarah Calder, 33, lives in the small town of Calais, Me., where she works as production manager of her family-owned newspaper, *The Calais Advertiser*. Colonel Saleh responded to her ad 15 months ago, and proposed to her last November.

Ms. Calder also said that she was captivated by the sweet talk in his e-mail messages and phone calls. Sometimes he wrote to her 10 or 12 times a day. Other times, she said, he told her she wouldn't be hearing from him for a week or so. He had to go into the hills and chase terrorists.

It is unclear how tall Colonel Saleh is. Women who have met him told some of the others that he was 5-foot-9 or 5-10, and possi-bly didn't even qualify for tall personals. In his mushy e-mail mes-sages, he told the women he was 6–3 or 6–5.

Ms. Calder was expecting to meet him in person for the first time in the coming days, and she said he called her a few weeks ago and mentioned that he had shrunk to six feet tall because of repeated parachute jumps. "I was very wary," she said. "I found it strange."

She only learned about the colonel's antics on Saturday, after she came home from doing dog rescues and found 49 e-mail messages on her computer. "They were all pertaining to Kass," she said. "I cried and cried and was totally heartbroken."

She said some of the other women had received engagement rings and were actually planning weddings. She had been shopping for a wedding dress herself, but fortunately hadn't bought it yet. Like others, Ms. Calder had sent him presents. She even had the local elementary school create handmade Valentine's Day cards to mail to his unit. He later sent photographs of the troops enjoying the cards.

"He's a sick individual who deserves jail time," she said.

She recognizes that it seems absurd to agree to marry someone whom you had never met in person, to trust a relationship built on e-mail messages and trans-Atlantic phone calls. But she said you had to be there and feel the seductive pull of his flowery words.

"We are not a group of stupid, naïve women," she said. "We are bright, intellectual, professional women. I can't tell you how much he wooed us with his words. He made us feel like goddesses, fairy princesses, Cinderellas. We had all found our Superman, our knight in shining armor."

N. R. Kleinfield

Seeking Relief, She Stepped out of Line

HOUSTON, Texas—A not-so-quick trip to the restroom has turned Denise Wells into something of a symbol for women's rights.

At a country-and-western concert here, Ms. Wells ducked desperately into a men's room, after the line at the women's room proved unbearably long. When she emerged (after being careful to put the toilet seat up, the way she found it), she was stopped by a police officer, given a $200 fine and escorted out of the arena, abandoning the third-row seat for which she had paid $125.

It seems a city law says women, no matter how needy or polite, cannot use the men's bathroom. Nor can men use the women's restroom.

Ever since, Ms. Wells has been Topic A on radio call-in shows and television man-and-woman-on-the-street interviews here. Opinion is almost unanimously on her side.

Her lawyer has received nearly 60 offers from women willing to testify on her behalf, saying that they, too, have sought relief in the men's room. Other callers have offered to pay her fine, but her lawyer, Valorie Davenport, who is also her sister, says that will not be necessary.

"I don't intend to lose," she said. "This is too important."

In Houston, as in most cities, there are rules about how many toilets there need to be in public places. For a long time these laws allowed a higher total of toilets and urinals in men's rooms than there were toilets in women's rooms because it was believed that more men than women attended large gathering places for sporting events and conventions. But then researchers actually did studies and found that this theory was not always right—lots of women attend conventions and sporting events. Not only that, because women's "plumbing" is different, it often takes them longer to use the toilet, so they actually need more toilets, not fewer.

So the code was changed—but it only applies to buildings built after 1985. Ms. Wells happened to be in a building which was built in 1975.

She and a friend arrived at a George Strait concert early, and Ms. Wells decided to use the restroom. But she went back to her seat, she said, after finding a line, more than 30 people long, snaking out the door.

"I decided to wait until the concert started," she said in an interview. "I figured all those women would go away by then."

Instead, when she returned to the restroom 20 minutes after the concert began, the line had nearly doubled. While her first trip had been a precaution, she said, this time she "really needed" to use the facilities. Standing in the slowly moving line, she saw a man enter the men's room across the way with his date. "I just followed them in," she said. She said she and the other woman, whom she does not know, cupped their hands like blinders around their eyes as they passed the urinals and entered stalls.

As they left, she said, a police officer clapped them each on the shoulder, gave them $200 citations and told them to leave immediately.

The police chief and the Mayor of Houston—both of whom

were women when this happened—could not be reached to be asked whether they had ever considered such a crime.

Ms. Wells has received support from all parts of the community, although many men point out that any man who walked into a crowded women's room would be in a lot more trouble than Ms. Wells.

Ms. Davenport said her plan was to "argue necessity as our first line of defense," adding, "What do they expect women to do?"

In addition, she said, she will argue that Ms. Wells did not in fact violate the city ordinance. Ordinance 72-904, passed in 1972, says, "It shall be unlawful for any person to knowingly and intentionally enter any public restroom designated for the exclusive use of the sex opposite to such person's sex . . . in a manner calculated to cause a disturbance."

Ms. Wells said she did not enter the men's room in any such manner. "I wasn't disruptive," she said. "I was embarrassed to death."

Lisa Belkin

CHECK PLEASE, AND FOR YOU, HERE'S MY BILL

NEW YORK, N.Y.—To hear Ethan Casey's side of the story, he is a man with a golden bag. Mr. Casey carried this very special bag—a knapsack that he used as a briefcase—when he went to eat lunch at Nicola Paone, a fancy Italian restaurant. Mr. Casey, who is a writer, checked the bag and had his lunch.

After lunch, the bag was missing from the coat room. The manager of the restaurant, Franco Alfonso, apologized and offered to replace it. "He said he had a couple of books and a passport in it," Mr. Alfonso said. "I told him I'd ask our insurance company to cover the loss. I figured it would be a couple of hundred dollars."

Two weeks later, a four-page letter arrived from Mr. Casey listing his losses and directing that a check be sent to his home in Colorado Springs. "I'm glad that you have insurance to cover this, and I appreciate your honorable offer to reimburse my losses and costs," he wrote.

The expense account began modestly, with "Items stolen (replace-ment costs)," a list that included the bag itself ($100), a watch ($150), a Swiss Army knife ($75), books ($50), AA batteries ($10) and a back issue of *Newsweek* ($20). Twenty dollars for an issue of *Newsweek* might seem high, but that was a bargain compared with the rest of the letter.

"The task of getting new documents has been tedious and time-consuming," Mr. Casey wrote, referring to his lost passport and other documents. "In addition to causing me to miss a scheduled interna-tional flight, it forced me to stay in one place for a full week and kept me from attending to much of my usual business. I was unable to make several major business telephone calls."

Mr. Casey valued his "Wasted week / forgone business growth" at $2,000. He tacked on another $2,100 for his time spent ("@ $150/hr.") replacing the documents, plus $1,250 to cover living and local transportation expenses during the week of waiting, plus $728 for new plane tickets. Under "Lost business—Southeast Asia and Seattle," Mr. Casey described the loss of a "taped interview for arti-cles for which I expected to receive $2,000" and "papers I needed in order to write another article for which I expected $1,000." But these were trivial compared with the loss of a "thick pile of business cards from recent business trips." The cards were "crucial" to his work but "not easily replaceable."

"It's impossible to know exactly how much the new business rela-tionships they represented could have been worth to me," he wrote. But he managed to come up with some figures.

"In order to reestablish these contacts, I would need to return to Thailand, Burma and Cambodia," Mr. Casey wrote. "Conservatively, I estimate the need to spend two weeks in Southeast Asia and one week in Seattle. Consistent with the standards of business travel, I require a per diem of $200." Besides the $4,200 in per-diem allowances, he required several plane tickets, including a $1,200 one to Bangkok.

Anyone else might have ended with that grand flourish, but Mr. Casey went on to close on a quieter note. He smoothly changed the tempo in a new section devoted to odds and ends: "I will have to repay $17.42 to my father for shipping a certified copy of my birth certificate to me overnight, $12.25 to Oconomowoc High School in Oconomowoc, Wisconsin, to ship a certified copy of my high school transcript overnight, and $37.20 to a friend who shipped me other needed identity documents overnight."

At the bottom of the fourth page, the expense account came to an elegantly terse conclusion: "TOTAL $14,641.87."

Mr. Alfonso had a strong suspicion that his insurance company would not be mailing out a check for that amount, but he did not bother arguing with Mr. Casey. "I just passed the letter to our insurance company as soon as I got it," Mr. Alfonso said. "As far as I know, nothing's happened with it."

Did Mr. Casey really expect anyone to pay his bill? He did not respond to several phone messages and e-mail messages from me over the past month, so I don't know. Maybe he has been busy collecting business cards in Southeast Asia. Or perhaps he has been working on his next expense account.

John Tierney

A Long Subway Ride

NEW YORK, N.Y.—At 6 A.M. yesterday, a 17-year-old Brooklyn high school student named Harry Beck got on the subway.

If you are reading this before noon today, there is a good chance that Harry Beck is still on the subway, probably beneath Brooklyn or Queens, badly in need of sleep, with a sore back, a weak cellphone battery, a ringing in his ears and a subway map on which most of the lines have been inked over in blue ballpoint pen.

The pen marks mean that Mr. Beck has traveled these lines sometime during the previous 24 hours, and if he is lucky—if he has not been stranded in a stalled train or met up with bullies or fallen asleep on a bench at Coney Island—he will be close to marking off the last line on the map, and ending a very, very long trip.

Most people take the train to get to work. Mr. Beck is taking it, more or less, to get to college. In truth, there were easier or fancier research projects he could have done to complete his senior project

at his high school in Brooklyn Heights. But Mr. Beck loves everything about the subway. He even runs his own subway Web site,
www.nycrail.com, and in his bedroom, plugged into the wall, is a
real, working subway signal.

So, he thought, *really* ride the subway—all 468 stations, about
230 route miles, 30 to 40 hours, Van Cortlandt Park to Rockaway
Park, with everything in between—and see if someone would give
him school credit for it, too.

"I mean, some kids are writing about French cuisine or 'This is
me going skiing every weekend at my country house,'" he said yesterday, in Hour 4 of the project. "I like riding the subway. So why
can't I do that?"

By noon yesterday, he was getting a little tired. He had tried to
get a good night's sleep the night before the trip, but he was far too
excited and finally drifted off at 4 A.M., an hour before he had to get
up. "I can't believe I'm doing this, actually, now that I think about
it," he reported at about Hour 6, sitting on a 2 train, across from a
woman watching him suspiciously as he wrote in his subway note-
book. "I mean, what a weird thing to do."

Mr. Beck does not look the part of what transit workers call
"foamers," their word for people who love the subway so much that
they appear rabid when discussing it. He has long, black, rock 'n' roll
sideburns and was traveling with a Weezer CD in his portable stereo
yesterday, packed into his green knapsack along with $27 in cash,
two bottles of water, gum, breath mints, nose drops, eye drops, a
radio scanner, gloves, a cell phone and his typed-out travel plan.

Asked to describe himself, he said: "I'm not king popularity, but
I'm not a loner either, like some subway guys. I'm not getting beat
up in school or anything because I like subways." His physics
teacher, Flo Turkenkopf, confirmed this. She says he knows there
are things he loves that make him a geek, "but he has a sense of
humor about it all."

The school's administrators and Mr. Beck's parents had less of a
sense of humor about his plans to skip two days of school to ride the
subways.

But they were eventually persuaded after Mr. Beck explained the valuable lessons he would be learning in sociology and urban affairs. Plus, he agreed to schedule in lunch and dinner breaks and have a teacher ride along with him overnight.

Reached last night by cell phone somewhere on the L train, Mr. Beck reported that he was faring well, that he had passed through about 230 stations or almost half and, as a bonus, had seen many good-looking young women on their way home at dinner time.

Next, he said, he was headed back to Brooklyn for his own dinner at his house. "You know, for my mom," he said. "To calm her down."

Randy Kennedy

Luxurious Lookout for the Parade

NEW YORK, N.Y.—If things go the way the police say they will, something like 2.5 million people will clog the streets to watch the Macy's Thanksgiving Day Parade tomorrow. Roughly 60 million more will take in the festive event on television. And 90 of them will watch it from the windows of Julie and David Tobey's apartment.

For anyone reading this who is going to the Tobeys', they wanted to point out that 8:30 A.M. will be plenty early enough. The parade starts at 9, a couple of blocks north of their building. One year, someone showed up at 7:45 and Julie Tobey was still in bed. It was an entirely unnecessary inconvenience.

The Tobeys live in the San Remo apartment building, at 146 Central Park West, between 74th and 75th Streets. There are any number of good reasons to be thankful one lives in the San Remo— it's hard to beat the neighborhood, and there's always a chance of seeing Steve Martin or Steven Spielberg in the elevator—but on

Thanksgiving, if one's apartment faces the park, the best reason is an unimpeded view of the parade without being trampled and with tastier food than the oversize pretzels sold by the street vendors.

And so it has become a cherished holiday custom for dozens of people who live in the San Remo, not to mention in so many of the apartments lining the parade route along Central Park West, to have relatives, friends and occasional interlopers converge on their homes to witness the marching bands and majorettes and Barney. For many years, the San Remo residents even got to admire one of their own out there. Eugene Tonkonogy, who lives in the building, marched in the parade for many years as a volunteer clown. He relented three years ago. He decided he was too old. He was 90. The Tobeys' party, continuous for 17 years, built onward and upward slowly. The Tobeys have no children of their own. The first year, the 8-year-old daughter of a friend asked if she could pretty please come by to see the parade. She came with her parents. Three people. She returned the following year, and brought some friends. Ten people. Then the Tobeys invited some of their other friends. Twenty-five people. Then other acquaintances started to call and ask if they could come by. Ninety people. "People bring their grandparents," Ms. Tobey said. "Or they bring their neighbors. Or they borrow children."

On 364 days of the year, New Yorkers want to be as high up in a building as possible. Today, for those in the San Remo, low is best.

Among the residents, there is a consensus, at least a consensus among those who live on the seventh floor, that seven is pretty much the perfect height. That is the height at which the balloons float past. When Superman flies past, you can practically step out your window and climb onto his back. The Tobeys feel seven is unquestionably best. The Tobeys live on seven.

Marjorie and David Silverman have little doubt that three is actually a much better floor. That's right, they live on three. They moved into the San Remo 10 years ago with two young children. Somehow it never occurred to them that the Thanksgiving Day parade went directly past their windows. They were very abruptly made aware of this when they were awakened their first Thanksgiving by bands that sounded as if they were bounding through their living room. "After that, we realized that it was sort of our obligation to have a parade party," Ms. Silverman said.

The parties are ostensibly for the children, but the critical word is ostensibly. Kathy and James Goodman, who live on seven, used to invite all the classmates of their daughter, Laura, each Thanksgiving, which naturally also meant siblings and those dreaded escorts known as parents. After fourth grade, Laura's interest in Big Bird and Kermit began to flag. Now that she has started college, it is nonexistent.

Her mother's appreciation of the parade, however, remains strong. Hence the Goodmans continue to invite friends over, though the quantity has diminished to about two dozen from more than 100 in past years. Among the regulars is a woman who grew up in the apartment but now lives on the 24th floor, where the parade is best enjoyed with the Hubble telescope. "Laura will be here, too," Ms. Goodman said, "but she'll probably sleep through it."

Mr. Goodman finds it difficult to relax entirely during these parade parties, which is understandable. Being art dealers, the Goodmans have a fair amount of art on display in the apartment. Particularly fragile pieces are stowed away, but much of it remains where it always is. Yet nothing has ever been damaged, and one year there were 120 people. "Nobody has even spilled their Bloody Mary on the rug," Ms. Goodman said.

The one clear reminder of the event is on the windows. "Thousands of tiny handprints, greasy ones, on all the windows throughout the apartment," Ms. Goodman said.

Getting to see the parade so well can become addictive. Withdrawal can be agonizing. A probably spurious story that floats around the San Remo is that when longtime owners sold their low apartment looking out on Central Park West, a condition of sale was that they and their friends be permitted to return the next Thanksgiving to watch the parade.

One of the genuinely gratifying things about having a crowd over to watch the parade is that often you get to meet people you had never expected to meet. Invitees mention to their own friends where they are going Thanksgiving morning, and suddenly those friends are in the back seat going, too. One year, someone took Pepe

Navarro, known as the David Letterman of Spain, to visit the Tobeys, who found him rather interesting. Another year a Welsh cabaret singer came with someone or other, and willingly sang for an hour after the parade.

So many people are coming to so many parties that sometimes the guests are mixed up. One year there were three people wandering around the apartment of the Silvermans, who invite only people they know. He thought they were her friends. She thought they were his friends. Actually, they were supposed to be going to a party on five. By the time they figured that out, they decided to just stay where they were. "They were lovely people," Ms. Silverman said.

Alas, a few San Remo residents with unbeatable views have had to forgo their tradition this year. Mady and Sandy Harman live on the second floor, with a normally exquisite view of the parade. This year, however, scaffolding to enable waterproofing work has been erected outside the building and it completely blocks their windows. Ms. Harman wrote to the co-op board to see if it could be dismantled for the parade, but she was told it would be too costly. And so when the 50 or so people who normally came to the Harmans' party began calling this year, they were advised that there would be nothing to come to.

Ms. Harman is having her brother over with his wife and three children, but she doesn't know how they will see the parade. She asked one of her upstairs neighbors if they could go there, but was told they already had too many people. The Harmans and their guests might have to watch it on television.

The building itself has had to prepare for the onslaught. With so many people thronging the sidewalks outside, there is concern that the building's shrubbery will be trampled, and that parade watchers might try to clamber onto the window ledges and fall and hurt themselves. Thus protective wooden barricades were put up along the facade. The front entrances will be locked during parade hours and the number of doormen and security people increased to 11 from the usual 5.

"Literally, at 6 in the morning, when you're asleep, you start to hear this buzz in the street," said Jane Ekstein, who lives on the 10th floor facing 75th Street. "People are already gathering for the parade. By 8 o'clock, you can't get out onto the block."

Residents with dogs, of which there are quite a few, go out the normally closed side entrances and encourage their pets to take care of business earlier than normal.

"Normally, if you walk from one end of the building to the other, it would take you 20 or 30 seconds," said George Caballero, a San Remo doorman who has worked the last 10 Thanksgivings. "On this day, it would take you 5 to 10 minutes, at least."

John Healy, the San Remo's resident manager, sent out a memo on Monday to residents reminding them to leave lists of guests with the doormen. He estimated that 700 to 800 guests would show up tomorrow, more than on any other day of the year. The residents were told to instruct their guests to use the side doors or the service entrances, which lead into the basement. "Though sometimes they get lost in the basement," said Latife Mardin, who with her husband, Arif, has been having friends over for 23 years. "It's tricky down there."

In his memo, Mr. Healy also warned residents not to park their cars on the street too close to Central Park West. He noticed last year that some paradegoers climbed atop parked cars to see better. The roofs of some of the cars collapsed.

After being hosts to a battalion of people to watch the parade, the San Remo dwellers often have to tidy up hurriedly for the second shift, the relatives and friends arriving for Thanksgiving dinner. Some residents, however, simply don't have the stamina to pursue any more entertaining.

"By the time the parade people leave, I'm ready to collapse," Ms. Tobey said. "Thank God, someone always invites us to their place for dinner."

N. R. Kleinfield

A Very Big Debt

SAN ANTONIO, Tex.—More than 200 years ago, a wealthy Pennsylvania merchant named Jacob DeHaven lent $450,000 to the Continental Congress to rescue the troops at Valley Forge. That loan was apparently never repaid.

So Mr. DeHaven's descendants are taking the United States Government to court to collect what they believe they are owed. The total: $141.6 billion in today's dollars if the interest is compounded daily at 6 percent, the going rate at the time. If compounded yearly, the bill is only $98.3 billion.

The thousands of family members scattered around the country say they are not being greedy. "It's not the money—it's the principle of the thing," said Carolyn Cokerham, a DeHaven on her father's side, who lives here in San Antonio.

"You have to wonder whether there would even be a United

States if this man had not made the sacrifice that he did," she said. "He gave everything he had."

The Federal Government, on the other hand, says the money is very much the issue. A United States Claims Court judge in Washington agreed with them, ruling that the statute of limitations—the amount of time that can pass before it is too late to sue about something—expired at least a century ago. But the family appealed that ruling, saying it was unconstitutional.

Unofficially, a Treasury spokesman said: "Yeah, we'll take it seriously, but they aren't going to win. You can't believe for a minute that anyone is going to get that kind of money."

The descendants say that they are willing to be flexible about the amount of a settlement and that they might even accept a heartfelt thank-you or perhaps a DeHaven statue. But they also note that interest is accumulating at $190 a second.

"None of these people have any intention of bankrupting the Government," said Jo Beth Kloecker, a lawyer from Stafford, Tex., who has taken the case in exchange for a share of any proceeds. "They understand about the deficit. But they want some acknowledgment of what Jacob DeHaven did."

What Mr. DeHaven did was respond to a desperate plea in 1777 from George Washington, the commander-in-chief of the Continental Army, when it looked as if the Revolutionary War was about to be lost. One of nine children in a wealthy family of merchants and landowners, Mr. DeHaven was living in Pennsylvania on farmland adjoining the Valley Forge campgrounds when Washington spent the winter there in 1777–78.

The soldiers were short of food, clothing, shelter and ammunition. General Washington sent a plea asking for money and saying that without it the Army would starve.

Mr. DeHaven was among those who responded. He lent the Government $50,000 in gold and what his descendants estimate to be another $400,000 in supplies. Because of this loan, they say, the Continental Army survived the winter at Valley Forge. When the war was over, Mr. DeHaven apparently tried several times to collect what was owed to him.

His relatives think he was offered Continental money for his loan certificate and that he held out for gold. In the early years of this country it sometimes seemed that the new government might not be around for too long and so Continental dollars were notoriously worthless, leading to the expression at the time that something was "not worth a Continental."

Mr. DeHaven died penniless in 1812 and is believed to be buried in Swedeland, Pa., in a family cemetery. He had no children of his own, so his sisters and brothers and their children and grandchildren are his legal heirs.

He was so poor when he died that there was nothing for them to inherit. But he did leave behind his story, and it was handed from one generation to the next. Every decade or two there has been an attempt by someone in the growing clan to collect the debt. Many of these efforts were carried out independently, with one branch of the family not knowing that another branch had tried and failed a decade earlier and in another part of the country.

In 1910, a branch of the family in Huntsville, Ala., hired lawyers to investigate the claim. Though the lawyers concluded that enough evidence existed to substantiate that the money was still owed, no suit was brought.

In the 1920's, President Calvin Coolidge told Congress that he thought the loan, then calculated at $4 million, should be repaid. In 1966, Representative Tom Pelly of Washington State introduced a resolution to repay $50,000 in settlement to the family, but the bill died in committee.

The latest attempt is thought to be the first time that the case has been brought to a court, rather than to Congress or Federal agencies. The suit began in January 1988 when Thelma Weasenforth Luunas of Stafford, Tex., a DeHaven on her father's side, approached Ms. Kloecker. Mrs. Luunas had promised her father shortly before he died that she would do her best to recover the loan—or, if she couldn't do that, to try to verify that the legend was true.

Ms. Kloecker consulted the Texas Commerce Bank in Houston to determine what the amount owed would be. The Continental Congress offered 6 percent interest on loans at that time; thus, the total, compounded daily, was calculated to be $141.6 billion in March 1989 when the suit was filed.

Then Ms. Kloecker began by searching for other descendants, and for any documents they might have, through advertisements and publicity in papers throughout the country. Responses have been received from more than 800 people, all of whom had been reared on the story of the loan, and they said they were amazed to find that someone else had heard it too. Many were from Pennsylvania, but letters and photocopied documents came from as far away as Italy and Hawaii.

Charles DeHaven, a pastor in New Braunfels, Tex., said his father first told him about the loan while he was studying the American Revolution in the fifth grade. "He told me, 'Someday, someday, the DeHaven family will be known for what it really did,'" he said.

Lisa Belkin

Shop till Eggs, Diapers and Toothpaste Drop

WASHINGTON, D.C.—It looks like a 7-Eleven in a box.

Early this morning, as the restaurants and clubs were shutting down in the Adams Morgan neighborhood here, a young waiter named Rick Roman joined a crowd gawking at the new attraction on the sidewalk: an 18-foot-wide vending machine.

Mr. Roman looked through the glass at the dozens of products—bottles of olive oil and milk, cartons of eggs, chicken sandwiches, paper towels, detergent, diapers, pantyhose, toothpaste, DVDs—and realized what he absolutely had to take home at 12:15 A.M. After he inserted a $10 bill and punched numbers on a screen, the crowd watched a metal bin rise to collect a package of razor blades from one shelf and a can of shaving cream from another.

One bystander muttered about "dehumanizing technology," but most oohed approvingly as the bin swung back to deposit the razors and cream in front of Mr. Roman. The machine even provided a plastic bag.

"It's pretty cool," Mr. Roman said. "Whoever made this is a genius. A guy in the store can make a mistake or give you a hard time, but not the machine. I definitely prefer the machine to a person."

This machine, the Shop 2000, is the only one operating in America. Some locals call it an eyesore, but others are happily posing for photos in front of it, and in its second week of operation, more than a few people are feeding it their cash and credit cards. If the test in Washington goes well, its manufacturer predicts a new era in convenience for Americans, as do rivals working on similar machines.

These kiosks, known as automated convenience stores (a better name might be RoboShop), are similar to multipurpose vending machines already operating in Japan and some cities in the Netherlands, Belgium and other European countries where labor is expensive and real estate is scarce. Those constraints are now being felt by American retailers. A study by the National Association of Convenience Stores suggests that a shortage of labor will be one of the industry's biggest problems in coming years.

"With this machine, you eliminate most of your labor costs as well as problems with theft," said Hettie Herzog, president of the machine's manufacturer, Automated Distribution Technologies of Exton, Pa. "Plus it goes into a small space. A typical convenience store takes up 2,500 square feet, but for this you need only 200. It's perfect for places that get a lot of foot traffic—busy sidewalks, dormitories, train stations, office buildings."

Ms. Herzog, who got the idea for her machine from one in Belgium selling groceries, tested it last year at a gas station in York, Pa. Drivers there did not provide enough business, but there were better results at a test at a parking lot near Howard University here this year, and she predicted strong sales from pedestrians now walking past the machine at the edge of a parking lot at a corner of 18th and California Streets in the city's northwest section.

The prices at the machine—$1 for a can of soup, $2 for a half-gallon of milk, $4 for a box of Cheerios—are in line with those at nearby convenience stores, although the selection is limited. Ms.

Herzog said her machine can stock about 200 products, less than a tenth of what is found in a typical convenience store.

"You can track sales remotely by dialing the machine's computer to find out exactly what's left of each item," she said. "If the machine stops or has a problem, it will call your pager and e-mail you."

This machine is being greeted cautiously by operators of traditional vending machines, as is a drive-through automated store under development by another company.

"Automated C-Store: Vending's Partner or Competitor?" was the headline of a recent article in the trade journal Automatic Merchandiser. Industry veterans note that there have been unsuccessful efforts to move beyond the "four C's"—candy, coffee, cold drinks, cigarettes.

The Keedoozle, a self-service grocery store using a conveyor belt, failed in the 1930's. A more successful predecessor, the Horn & Hardart Automat offering hot food, was supplanted by fast-food franchises.

"One reason full-line vending machines have not swept the United States to date is that we have had a large population of entrepreneurial immigrants eager to operate convenience stores," said Timothy Sanford, editor of the trade journal *Vending Times*. "But it's getting very hard to find capable sales staff, and it doesn't make sense for them to spend valuable time selling simple items that don't require their expertise."

RoboShops have advantages, he said. "You don't need bathroom space for employees and aisles for customers. You don't need to worry about someone pulling a gun on a clerk. The public needs to get used to these kinds of stores, but I think it's inevitable that they will. People are already accustomed to automatic teller machines and self-service gas pumps. When they know what they want, they want to get it without waiting in line and worrying about whether the clerk's had a bad day."

Those attitudes were evident in a survey by the National Association of Convenience Stores. When asked which factors affected their decision to shop in a convenience store, people ranked "friendly, helpful service" well below "convenient location" and "fast in and out of store." Way down the list, in 13th place, was "pleasant store ambience."

Still, some people watching the machine defended stores with clerks. "I'm concerned about the people this is going to put out of work," said David Bottoroff, an editor. "It's shockingly inhumane, and it's also an eyesore. I'd much rather see a storefront here than this ugly box."

Other late-night machine-watchers shared his feelings and complained about lazy Americans' obsession with convenience, but the critics seemed to be few. "Awesome" was the typical review. "Like something from the future!" shouted the leader of a group heading home from a bar.

Even Mr. Bottoroff paid the machine a compliment. He did not approve of it, he said, but since there were no competing stores open on the block at this hour, there might come a night when he buys a DVD or popcorn or something. "I have to admit it's convenient," he said.

John Tierney

A TOWN THAT TIME, AND ALSO TREES, FORGOT

NOTREES, Tex.—In an act of hope, determination or just plain boredom, Kim Baumguardner and her husband, Sam, are planting trees in this dusty West Texas town. Two tiny shrubs, all but hidden by barbed wire, sit in the center of a newly purchased plot next to the Baumguardner home. Mrs. Baumguardner's best friend used to live there. Recently she moved away.

Nearly everyone has moved away from Notrees (pronounced No Trees). Old-timers recall that there were once several hundred people here; even as recently as the last census there were 338. Now there are 41 or 42, depending on whether you count Jennifer Whitehead's newborn son, who has not yet come home from the hospital in Odessa, 26 miles to the west.

The entire town spans several hundred feet on both sides of Highway 302. There are a gas station, a post office and two side streets. There used to be several oil-drilling camps here too. But over the years they left, and their employees had no reason to remain. Now nearly everyone who lives in Notrees works for the Shell Oil plant on the edge of town.

"I say they should rename it Nopeople," quipped Millsie King, who has worked in the Notrees post office for 12 years but lives in Odessa. "There are trees—some, at least. But there aren't no people."

There were no trees in Notrees when it was named back in 1944. The Post Office Department had told Postmaster C. J. Brown to find a descriptive name, and so he did.

Virtually all the couple of dozen or so trees that are here today, planted by residents over the years, are either dead or dying, victims of dust storms, brush fires and cloying oil fumes.

Blackie Robertson chopped off the tops of the trees outside his house last month, because they were dying for lack of water anyway. Only the trunks and the amputated branch stumps remain, standing in stark outline against a flat landscape. Birds crowd onto the telephone line near his home, having no other place to sit.

Mr. Robertson, who runs a cattle ranch here, has been a Notrees resident for 24 years and remembers when the town had a cafe, a beer hall and a school. A former bronco rider, he still wears his spurs, even in his carpeted living room. The smaller his hometown gets, the better he likes it. "I'd rather be off 20 minutes from any town," he said. "When you get stuffed up around people, it's like Peyton Place."

As for Mrs. Baumguardner, she was born here 25 years ago, when her father worked for Shell. She, her three children and her husband, a Shell employee, live in the house where she grew up. She has been outside Texas once, for a vacation in New Mexico.

What's new in Notrees? Well, the service station reopened last month, much to everyone's relief. It had been closed for three months, until the previous owner sold it to J&J Trucking, the only other business for miles. Now Mr. Robertson does not have to go to the tiny nearby hamlet of Goldsmith for his Camel Light 100's.

Also new is the "for sale" sign in front of Charlie and Sybil Lovelace's home. Nine years ago they paid $72,000 for the house, the only two-story structure in town, and they say they will be happy if they can sell it for $40,000. Mr. Lovelace worked at the Shell plant for 25 years, but, having retired now, he wants to move. "We want to live where there's drugstores and hospitals and other things people need when they're very mature," Mrs. Lovelace said.

And, of course, there is Mrs. Baumguardner's garden—the two Italian blue cypresses she chose because they were "cute." She says she knows that other trees in Notrees are dying, but insists hers will be different. "The other ones are kind of deserted," says Mrs. Baumguardner, whose name, believe it or not, means "tree gardener" in German. "No one comes around to water them. No one cares about them."

She points proudly to the two mulberrys her father planted years ago, still thriving in the front yard, and to the cedar and the weeping willow growing happily out back. She has watered them once a week for as long as she can remember, and now she drags a hose to the plot next door and waters her new plants every other day.

"It's something that will last," she said.

Lisa Belkin

TRYING TO GET ALONG

FINALLY, AN INTEGRATED GEORGIA PROM

FORT VALLEY, Ga.—For 20 years, blacks and whites at the high school in this rural Georgia town sat side by side in classes and Key Club meetings, marched in the band together and wore the same black-and-gold uniforms on the football team.

But they couldn't go to the prom together.

Every spring—long after the days of segregation had ended nearly everywhere in the United States—the white students at Peach County High School danced to their music and crowned a white king and queen at their prom while the black students held a black prom and chose a black king and queen. Long after segregation was officially gone from this state and this country, the proms were still held in separate halls—even in separate towns.

"We knew it was wrong, but it was a tradition and people just went along with it," said Kristi Brewton, a black student at the high school.

All of that changed Saturday night. Two hundred black couples and white couples, girls in sequined sheaths and Scarlett O'Hara gowns, arm in arm with dates in tuxedos, floated into the school gymnasium to dance and compare corsages at the county's first integrated prom. (No king and queen were crowned this year.) It has taken years of cajoling and pressure from a small group of parents and students to get to this point in a part of Georgia where 10 other counties still hold segregated proms, and where segregated class reunions are not uncommon.

The push to do this came from the students—who said they were embarrassed by the tradition. "It's hard to explain when we go on vacation to California," said Ato Crumbly, a black senior. "I'd tell people about our prom and they would get a funny look on their face and ask, 'Do you have to drink from separate fountains, too?'"

Change has come remarkable slowly to Fort Valley, a town of 10,000 people in central Georgia divided by the railroad track and by race. Most blacks live south of the tracks, where the jail is; most whites live north of the track, where the school and most businesses are.

"Racism is still thick here," said Dr. Donnie Bellamy, chairman of the political science and history department at Fort Valley State College. "Decisions are made by whites and by the time blacks find out about it, it's too late."

Integration has been resisted here since the start of the civil rights movement. In the 1960's, several establishments shut down rather than permit blacks to fraternize with whites. The movie theater closed years ago, refusing to let blacks and whites sit together.

Even all these years later, the group of parents, teachers and students seeking to integrate the prom encountered similar resistance from the white School Superintendent and the predominantly white seven-member school board.

The parents' group first asked the board in 1986 to allow an integrated prom. The board voted against it, 5 to 2. The parents went to work on electing a new superintendent and some new board members. Finally the board voted 6 to 1 for an integrated prom.

And so it was not until 36 years after the Supreme Court ordered school desegregation that Kelly Kennedy, a white senior, and Kristi

Brewton, a black senior, would be the county's first black and white classmates able to go to the same prom. They have been friends since first grade.

They both spent all day Saturday planning and primping and running errands for the big day. Kelly took two baths and sat in her electric hair curlers, putting on coat after coat of red nail polish.

Kristi went to the beauty shop for finishing touches on her hair and capped her nails with pink polish. They compared notes on their dresses—Kelly would wear black sequins, Kristi white sequins—and waited nervously for their dates to arrive.

The previous year, they had both gone to their respective proms and reported back to each other about how the other race did things. This time it would be different. "Instead of saying I did this at my prom," Kelly said, "we can talk about what we did together at our prom."

Saturday's prom goers had not yet been born when the school was forced to integrate, and some felt a bit uneasy at being groundbreakers. "When I moved here from Missouri, I couldn't believe it," said Gerald Walker, 17, a junior escorting Tomia Palmer, a senior. "I thought all of this had been taken care of back in the civil rights days."

Watching the moonless evening unfold were parents, black and white, many of whom had resisted the idea and had never been to an integrated prom. They took turns taking pictures in the gym, beaming as their children danced and ate pretzels and peanuts.

"I looked out there and thought, 'This should have happened years ago,'" Mrs. Crumbly said. "I don't know what people thought would happen if we let our kids get together."

Dozens of alumni came to see how it went. "It's the most beautiful thing the county has ever done," said Amy Gay, a white 1988 graduate.

On the dance floor it was even more beautiful than that. "This is the missing link in our circle," said Kristi. "Now we can be one school. We're showing everybody that it's never too late."

Isabel Wilkerson

A Knife Divides Them

MONTREAL, Canada—Canada is proud that it is one of the world's most welcoming nations to immigrants, so tolerant that several major cities have populations where more than one-third of the people were born in other countries.

But Gurbaj Singh, a 12-year-old Sikh boy who immigrated here from a small village in the Punjab, learned the limits of Canadian tolerance in the schoolyard of his new elementary school.

While Gurbaj was playing basketball, his 4-inch kirpan—the ceremonial curved dagger Sikh men are obliged to wear at all times, even while sleeping—jostled loose and fell to the ground. A startled parent noticed the blade, and reported the incident to the principal.

Gurbaj found himself facing his principal, who ordered the boy to hand over his kirpan.

Since the age of 5, Gurbaj said, he has never taken off his kirpan, which in the Sikh faith symbolizes the sovereignty of man and serves as a reminder to go to the defense of others in distress.

So he walked out of school and went home instead, beginning a struggle that would test the limits of religious freedom in this society which is so proud of being free.

Gurbaj's act of conscience has caused him to miss months of school, and it has made him a celebrity of sorts here and as far away as India, while igniting months of radio talk show debate and fierce dueling editorials in both French and English language newspapers (both languages are spoken in different parts of Canada).

The case has been winding its way through the courts. A court ruled that Gurbaj could wear his blade to school as long as it was securely enclosed in a wooden sheath tied tightly shut and remained tucked under his shirt. But the government of Quebec—the French part of Canada, where Gurbaj lives—appealed that ruling.

"The maintenance of security in schools," said the Quebec justice minister, Paul Bégin, "requires zero tolerance for the carrying of knives."

Gurbaj and his family say that they will go all the way to the Supreme Court, if necessary, and that if they lose there they will be forced to move to either Ontario or British Columbia, provinces with large Sikh populations where schools do not prohibit kirpans.

"I cannot part with my kirpan because it is part of the obligation I accepted when I took my baptism," Gurbaj said in an interview. "I am determined to stand up for my rights."

Gurbaj has gone back to school. When the court first ruled he could return with his kirpan, he was met by dozens of angry parents, many of whom kept their children home for several days in protest. Accompanied by a police escort, Gurbaj was forced to endure a shower of racial and anti-immigrant insults from some of the adults.

He appeared remarkably composed under all that pressure, especially considering he is a boy of 12 in a new country. He has an easy wide smile and curls his brow thoughtfully before answering questions.

He appears to have blended his native and Canadian cultures, spending his spare time playing basketball and searching the Web on his computer in his bedroom, which has pictures of the sacred Sikh gurus and his kirpan collection. He wears his hair tied up in a scarf called the patka and, under religious law, promises never to shave, drink alcohol or eat meat.

He says he has never gotten into a fight, and would never think of using his kirpan as a weapon. "The kirpan is not a knife, it is a religious symbol," he said.

Clifford Krauss

DAUGHTER OF APARTHEID

TSAKANE, South Africa—For years, the country girl wished she could wiggle out of her skin and shed her color like the molting snakes that rustled through the green fields. It was the 1960's, and she was the daughter of white Afrikaners here who proudly supported the government's brutal system of apartheid and racial segregation.

But for Sandra Laing, it was hard to swallow the message of hate. Her birth certificate said she was white, but when she looked in the mirror, she saw a honey brown face framed by a halo of kinky-curly hair. A face anyone who looked at her would describe as black. "They loved me," she said of her parents. "But I knew I was different."

For a time, the Laings tried to ignore the trick of genetics and ignored the whispers about the African blood many suspected flowed through their veins. But by age 15, Sandra Laing had been expelled from her all-white school and disowned by her humiliated parents and her story had become one of the country's most publicized examples of a family destroyed by the crushing weight of apartheid.

The saga should have faded into the yellowing pages of forgotten newspapers. But one day, long after the fall of apartheid in South Africa, Ms. Laing drove home for the first time in nearly 30 years, accompanied by a documentary filmmaker, and what she saw became prime-time news. In the once segregated town of Piet Retief in Mpumalanga Province, she found a black farmer living in her parents' old house. At the school that had once rejected her, she met students black and white. One told her, "God has changed this world."

And in January, she saw her mother for the first time since 1973, in a tearful reunion that was splashed across the nation's newspapers.

But if Ms. Laing's story reflects the triumphs of a struggling democracy that has managed to overcome decades of racial hatred, it also shows the painful journeys of ordinary people who sometimes stumble along the new road toward racial reconciliation. Her two brothers, who have prospered in the white world, are still so ashamed of their sister that they refuse to see her or speak to her.

And so go race relations in this country, with tentative steps forward and tentative steps back, as whites and blacks, Indians and coloreds wrestle with the past. Six years after South Africa elected its first black president, the apartheid laws and racial classifications are long gone. Blacks are moving into white neighborhoods. Lovers exchange wedding rings across the color line in a country that once outlawed mixed marriages.

But here in this poor black township where she now lives, Ms. Laing has discovered that while much has changed, much has not. The history of apartheid still divides her family. In March, her brothers sent a letter to Ms. Laing, now 44, who was facing eviction here, and promised to help her buy food. But the money would come at an almost unspeakable cost.

She would receive their help, the letter said, only if she vowed never to see her 79-year-old mother again and only if she promised to keep quiet about her family history. At the time she heard from her brothers, she had managed to visit her mother twice.

She never answered the heartbreaking letter, but it is a measure of her isolation that she now treasures it, keeping it safe in a plain envelope tucked in her wardrobe. These days, she believes it may be one of the only tangible connections she will ever have to her family.

"I always thought after apartheid it would be all right," Ms. Laing said, her hands twisting nervously in her lap, her fingernails bitten to the quick. "I hoped my brothers would come looking for me," she said wistfully. "I still hope they will come."

She falls silent, maybe because she knows they will never come looking. Maybe because, as horrible as it may sound, she can almost understand how they feel. Even as she kissed her mother's wrinkled cheek when they saw each other for the first time six months earlier, she could still feel the unbearable distance between them.

"When I saw my real mother again, I was happy to see her, but it didn't feel right," Ms. Laing admitted quietly. "She's white and I'm dark. It just doesn't feel right."

Her older brother, Leon Laing, says he is sorry for the pain of the past, but he insists that history cannot be undone. The siblings will probably never know whether their family had a black ancestor somewhere, as some suspect, or whether their mother had an affair with a black man, as others believe.

But even in this new South Africa, Mr. Laing worries that his children would be humiliated if their white friends and neighbors suspected they had black African ancestry. So he pretends his little sister was never born and begs reporters to help him keep the secret.

"This story is 35 years old," Mr. Laing said, his voice growing ragged as he explained why he would not discuss his sister. "I've got my wife and kids to think of. You understand? I have to keep them safe."

It is hard to imagine now, but there was a brief time in Sandra Laing's life when color did not seem to matter. The South African Broadcasting Corporation, which aired the documentary on her life, recovered an old black-and-white video which was shot before she was expelled from school and before her brothers learned to view her with shame.

In the flickering, silent footage, Ms. Laing is a laughing little girl who races into her mother's arms, nestles close to her smiling father and cuddles her brother on her knee. But she was a brown child living in a white world and she inevitably tripped up against the country's apartheid laws.

Under the Population Registration Act, which was enacted in 1950 and repealed in 1991, every newborn baby was classified by race. Those classified as black or mixed-race—known as coloreds—could not live or study in white communities. It was under that law that Ms. Laing was expelled from her white school in 1966, when her schoolmates complained and the government reclassified her as black.

Her parents managed to reclassify her as white, taking blood tests to prove she was their child. But they disowned her when they caught her dating a black man. To live legally with the man she loved, Ms. Laing had to reclassify herself as colored and leave the white community. And the family slowly learned to live in two separate worlds, one white, one black.

Her father, Abraham, still not speaking to her, died in 1989. And her mother, Sannie, sits in a suburban nursing home just outside Pretoria, finding safety from history in silence and forgetfulness.

"I never see her, I never see her," Sannie Laing said recently, when a reporter asked about her only daughter.

When she was gently reminded that her daughter had visited twice, the silver-haired woman nodded slowly. "Oh, yes, yes," she said. "I can remember."

But she refuses to say more. The memories are too painful or too elusive, flickering in and out of her mind like fireflies on a warm summer night. And after so many years, Ms. Laing no longer has the courage to ask, How could you have ignored all my letters and phone calls? How could you have abandoned me for so many years?

Instead, Ms. Laing finds comfort in black townships, where she has lived since she left her white family, where people do not view her as an oddity.

Here, she is simply the friendly neighbor who tends the pink roses in her tiny garden and hangs fraying towels on the clothesline like other black women. "At home, I wished I was lighter like my family," she said. "Here, it's O.K. who I am."

But it is not an easy life. Ms. Laing is unemployed and her second husband, a machine operator, works only part time. The family struggles to pay the rent on their four-room house and often goes without bread or meat. Most weeks, she does not even have the 72 cents to make a 10-minute phone call to her mother.

She places her hopes for the future in her 12-year-old son, Steve, who plans to become a doctor in a country that no longer denies opportunities to blacks. He studies hard and mixes easily with the whites he meets in town. But when asked whether he will move into a white neighborhood or practice medicine in a white community someday, Ms. Laing shakes her head.

Her children will be safe, she says. They will not cross the line. "They know how I grew up," she said. "They will remain with black people."

Rachel L. Swarns

WHO WOULD KILL A TREE?

_____

AUSTIN, Tex.—This is a murder mystery. The victim is a tree.

Not just any tree, but a 500-year-old live oak, which Texans like to brag is "the most perfect tree in America." It is 50 feet tall. The branches reach out 127 feet. Its picture has hung in the Tree Hall of Fame in Washington.

It is revered because of a legend that is probably not true—that Stephen F. Austin made peace with the Indians in its shade. Anyway, that is why it is called the Treaty Oak. Marriages have been held under its canopy. Nearby cafes and office complexes have taken its name.

Now someone is trying to kill it. Someone who seems to know a lot about trees; enough to choose an obscure herbicide and pour it onto the roots. City tree experts are not certain the Treaty Oak will die, but they are not optimistic that it will live, either.

Ever since the damage was first noticed last month, the tree has become the city's biggest celebrity. A small hushed crowd gathers near it every day, dangling ornaments in its branches and leaving bouquets and get-well cards at its base.

"I've never seen anything like this," said John Giedraitis, a city forester. "But I've never seen someone try to murder a tree, either. Everybody loves trees, except when they drop on your house or something. This one was minding its own business."

The Treaty Oak stands in the center of a small, square plot ringed by benches and surrounded by a parking lot, an antique store and a row of homes. The park dates to 1937 when, in the middle of the Depression, schoolchildren saved their pennies to help the city buy the property. One of the requirements of the sale was that the tree would never be removed.

Today the park is ringed with yellow police tape. The ground is a mess of holes the size of coffee cans, which were made by soil-sample drills. It looks as though a gopher has been through.

It has been this way for several weeks, since the city Parks Department received a call saying the tree was not looking good. Its symptoms—the veins on each leaf were alive but the rest of the leaf was brown and dry—were those of chemical poisoning.

Tests found evidence of Velpar, an herbicide that inhibits photosynthesis and is used specifically to kill hardwood trees. The chemical was probably applied, in large amounts, more than three months earlier, according to the Texas Agriculture Department, which has ruled out accidental contamination from any source.

When he released the test results Max Woodfin, a spokesman for the department, said the choice of Velpar could only have been made by a canny killer. "You usually have to get it through an agricultural or chemical distributor," he said.

Right away, city foresters removed a six-inch-deep layer of soil at the tree's base, replaced it with clean soil and injected microbes to break down the Velpar. Then they waited for the second flush of growth that a tree puts out when its first leaves are contaminated.

The new leaves opened a few weeks later, all shiny and green. But soon they, too, were turning brown. "That means we didn't beat it," Mr. Giedraitis said.

The E. I. du Pont de Nemours & Company plant in La Porte,

Tex., where Velpar is made, has offered a $10,000 reward for information leading to the conviction of whoever is trying to murder the Treaty Oak.

"How dare someone misuse our product this way!" said Pat Getter, a spokesman for Du Pont's Southwestern office.

The Austin police have been getting in touch with all area suppliers of Velpar and say they have a suspect. But so far no one has been arrested and no motive has been established. There are theories, of course. Some believe a developer wanted to kill the tree to free the land. Others think a disgruntled city employee wanted a rather indirect form of revenge.

All over Austin—all over Texas, really—people are asking "why would anyone want to kill a tree?" Mary Taylor, of Waco, brought her granddaughter, Robin Hukill, of Tyler, to see the Treaty Oak. "You may be seeing something that won't be here when your grandchildren are growing up," Mrs. Taylor told Robin.

John Silverberg, an Austin pharmacist came by at lunch to "pay my respects." Joe Lynch, a construction worker, brought his camera "to get a picture while it's still here." A group of joggers, who changed their daily route so they could pass the tree, slowed their pace, looked pensive, then continued on. Robin Edger came, as he does every lunch hour, to talk softly to the branches.

"Come on, you can get through this," he told the tree.

"It works with my rhododendrons, why shouldn't it work with a tree?" asked the human standing nearby.

Another daily visitor is Mr. Giedraitis, who is particularly fond of this tree. The first bench to the right was where he proposed to his wife.

"I got down on one knee on the ground right there," he said, pointing to a spot now riddled with holes. "I thought it was a fitting symbol of our commitment to each other. I figured this thing's going to be here forever."

Lisa Belkin

The High Cost of Looking Like an All-American Guy

WEEHAWKEN, N.J.—In the days before he did the awful act, 20-year-old Parwinder Singh made two purchases that would have surely given him away had his father, Sukhdev, or mother, Kanwaljit, known. He bought a soft-brim, floppy hat and scissors from Rite-Aid, hiding both in his bedroom.

They realized that their only son, a taxi driver and college student, was upset, but didn't see how deep it went. The immigrant family is Sikh, a religion of India, and since Sept. 11, they have been gawked at everywhere they go. Sikhs consider hair as natural a part of the body as arms or legs, and Sikh men are not supposed to ever cut it. So they wear turbans to cover their long braids and their beards grow a foot or more.

Sikhs are not Muslim. Indeed, through history they have often battled Muslim empires. But to confused Americans they resemble Osama bin Laden, and late one September night that is what a half-dozen thugs in East New York, Brooklyn, screamed at Parwinder Singh, smashing three windows in his taxi with beer bottles. After that, the mother said Parwinder must stop working. For days he stayed indoors, but it made him feel fearful and hopeless. He saw only one way out. He would wake one morning, ready to do it. Then, the next morning he could not; he knew that his father would feel disgraced, and the young man had been raised to respect his father like a god. Finally his mind was firm. His father was at work driving a limousine, his sister was at high school. He locked the bathroom door and stared into the mirror. For five minutes, he stood frozen. Then he put the scissors to his throat and cut.

The black, wiry hair came off in clumps in his fist and fell over the sink and floor. The job took longer because tears blurred his vision. He cut only his beard; he figured he could wear the floppy hat over the braid. He saved as much beard as possible in a jewelry box, then used wet toilet paper to clean up the rest and flushed it away.

When his mother saw it, she began screaming in Punjabi. "She crying, 'What you did?'" he recalled, in English, his second language. "I say: 'If I live in this country I will do it. If I don't cut my hairs, Americans will kill me.' I thought if I cut it, no one will know who's this guy." He ran to his bedroom, locked himself in and cried. His father came home from work and pounded the door. "He beat me up," the son said. "Not with fists. He hits me in words. He was crying, 'Why you did it?'"

The whole family sat in his room and cried. His mother made no meal that night. "They keep asking, 'Why you did it?'" he said. "I said I have to, if I can live in this country." They said his father didn't cut his hair. "You older," Parwinder said. "You don't know it is hard to be young."

Next morning, before the others awoke, he returned to the bathroom and tried on the floppy brim hat. His bun was too high and the hat dangled on it. So he undid the two-foot braid, cut off a third of it, saving this hair in the box, too. He put on the hat again. It sat nicely on his head. He was crying; he really looked like an American guy.

They own a two-family house, and when his uncle, Balaka Singh, heard about this downstairs, he raged in Punjabi, "Kick him out of the house!" The uncle, a cabdriver, is a Sikh Youth of America vice president and, since Sept. 11, has been lecturing his people to hold to their customs despite all the hate crimes aimed at the half-million American Sikhs—including the murder of a gas station owner in Arizona. "Parwinder did not listen; I told our people not to cut their hair and my nephew does," the uncle recalled.

"What will people think at the Gurdawara?" he said of the Sikh temple.

The young man said he felt remorse and would never cut his hair again. This softened the uncle, who said: "I don't want him kicked out. But he is not a righteous person."

Every time Parwinder leaves the house now, his whole family asks him to wear his turban. A family friend, Harbhajan Singh, saw him at a restaurant in his floppy hat and said: "I was surprised. I did not recognize you as a Sikh."

In his cab, people look at his hack license photo, with the turban and the beard, and ask, "This is really you?"

His 4-year-old cousin, Jugraj, asked, "Why did you cut it?" Parwinder answered, "I got a hard time."

"You lie," the boy said. "You want to be American."

Parwinder is so shamed, he prays at his Temple only on Saturday now, when it is least busy and few will know him.

One recent night, as he left his house, his mother said: "You look like you're not our son. Please wear your turban."

And he answered, "Maybe in a few weeks."

Michael Winerip